THE BOOMERANG EFFECT

MALACHI WALKER

Quantity sales special discounts are available on quantity purchases by corporations, associations, and others. For details, contact the publisher at the address above.

Orders by U.S. trade bookstores and wholesalers. Email info@BeyondPublishing.net

The Beyond Publishing Speakers Bureau can bring authors to your live event. For more information or to book an event contact the Beyond Publishing Speakers Bureau speak@BeyondPublishing.net

The Author can be reached directly https://beyondpublishing.net/AuthorMalachiWalker

Manufactured and printed in the United States of America distributed globally by BeyondPublishing.net; Editor: S. Christina Walker; Book Cover Design: Panos Lampridis; Author Picture: Sam Gill; Cover Boomerang Graphic: Scott McGill/Shutterstock.com (used under liscense); Gold Boomerang Thrower graphics: Scott Maxwell/Shutterstock.com (used under liscense).

BEYOND
PUBLISHING

New York | Los Angeles | London | Sydney

10 9 8 7 6 5 4 3 2 1 978-1-947256-86-6

TABLE OF CONTENTS

Foreword   By Clint Gresham 06
                Seattle Seahawks Super Bowl XLVIII Champion

Introduction 10

Chapter 1   Get-Up or Give-Up? 17

Chapter 2   Boomerang Success Mindset 36

Chapter 3   Boomerang Mindset Teams 48

Chapter 4   Which Team Are You Throwing For? 58

Chapter 5   X-Use the Excuse 74

Chapter 6   Mindset Conditioning 92

Chapter 7   *BOOM!* 114

Chapter 8   Savage Not Average 126

Chapter 9   The Cheer-On Boomerang 142

Chapter 10   Your Face Is Speaking 158

Chapter 11   Take The Shot 168

Chapter 12   Shatter Up 184

To Mom and Dad

I could not have gotten a single word on these pages without your help, love and support. Mom, thank you so much for the countless hours you spent guiding, editing, encouraging, supporting and coaching me throughout this process. It was your prayers, patience and selfless love that brought me through those tough times and gave me the insight I needed to make this book so awesome. Dad, you are the man! Thanks for keeping the lights on and letting me borrow space in that little apartment.

FOREWORD

by *Clint Gresham*

*Seattle Seahawks Super Bowl XLVIII Champion,
International Speaker and Best-Selling Author of
"Becoming: Loving the Process to Wholeness."*

I was a wide-eyed and disoriented young man when I walked into the team meeting room at *Texas Christian University*. Even though I had spent the prior year at the *University of Oklahoma* trying to earn the starting role of long snapper for the powerhouse OU football program, I still found myself intimidated by the people in the room at TCU.

Things at OU hadn't ended well, and I never saw it coming. While being recruited by OU as a senior in high school, I was intoxicated by the "big school" football program. Adrian Peterson was going to be my teammate. I was going to play in BCS games. It might as well have been professional football. But it was those "bright lights" that blinded me as I chose to "walk-on" with the promise from the coaching staff that I would be put on scholarship after my first semester at OU.

Here was the gamble though...TCU had offered me a scholarship. They wanted me to be their long snapper for the next four years. But by that point, my heart (and most likely my ego) pulled me towards the big show in Norman, Oklahoma. I walked away from a scholarship because of the promise of what I thought was a bigger, better deal, and the words from coaches who I thought would follow through on what they promised.

With my first semester down, I waited to hear from my coach about my scholarship. He told me, "We want to see you through spring ball." When we finished spring ball he informed me again, "We want to see you through summer workouts and all of next season."

By this point, I had heard through the grapevine that OU was looking at bringing in another athlete to fill the role as their long snapper. They had told the media they didn't have anyone on the team who could do the job. It was devastating. I had never worked so hard for something in my life. I felt defeated, un-wanted and irrelevant.

After talking with my dad, who was an absolute God-send during that painful time, we decided it would be best to take my talent south to *Texas Christian University* (the team I had turned down while being recruited as a senior in high school). And even though I had turned them down after they had offered me a scholarship and a guarantee to start, TCU still had a place for me.

The meeting room was buzzing with anticipation of the 2006 season as Gary Patterson, head coach for TCU, walked through the door. He was a bull-dog. The kind of man you always want to have on your side. He started to address the team before training camp and the veins in his neck began to swell. The raspiness of his voice told the tale that he was the kind of football coach who drove his vocal chords to their limits. He was a man who didn't need to demand respect, because he already had it.

After the initial statements about what the culture of that season's team was going to look like, Coach P changed gears. You could tell he hated addressing the topic, but he knew it had to be done. (The mark of a real man is talking about the hard stuff!) Coach took a breath, looked us in the eyes and said, "You are only allowed to quit once in this program."

The statement didn't make sense to me at first, but as the year progressed it began to mean more and more to me. I had no idea that statement would become a core message of the man I would become. The statement was sort of like America's stance regarding negotiating with terrorists. We don't do it. If we do, it would set the precedent that allows for that type of behavior to become common.

What Coach P was saying to all of us that day was that the program would not tolerate young men who want to be selfish. But even more than quitting being a sign of selfishness, quitting is a habit. It's a deadly habit that I didn't even know I was addicted to.

Throughout that season, I started doing some soul searching. I began looking back on my life and seeing, time after time, moments that I quit because things got hard. I quit baseball because I wanted to hang out with a girlfriend who was abusive. I quit basketball because I wanted to play video games. I quit relationships with people because they wouldn't do things my way. And I quit at OU, because I got my feelings hurt. That day in the team meeting room at *Texas Christian University*, Clint Gresham got a wakeup call that if he was ever going to make anything of his life, he had better "quit quitting."

Four years later, I'd graduated from TCU and was working out with the *New Orleans Saints*. I was sitting in a hotel room and got a knock on the door. It was one of the team scouts and he let me know that the head coach, Sean Payton, wanted to talk to me. I had no idea what was about to happen. As I walked into the lonely room with Sean at the table, he looked at me with a sense of somberness and informed me they were letting me go. They didn't have enough room on the roster. I was heartbroken.

I drove back to Fort Worth, Texas that day feeling those old feelings of wanting to throw in the towel. It's incredibly emotional and humiliating when you feel like a failure. But in the back of my mind, I heard the voice of my college head coach ringing through my head saying, "Don't quit." In that moment, I had to choose my mindset and because I chose correctly, the "Boomerang-Effect" took care of the rest.

Like Malachi says, I chose to set my mind on "Get-Up" not "Give-Up" so I could get the right result. And the next day I received a call from the *Seattle Seahawks*. They told me they had a flight booked for me that night in first class, for practice the next morning.

I was awestruck. The right mindset had boomeranged back to me and I ended up arriving in Seattle and spending six seasons in one of the most incredible organizations in the world! I had the privilege of playing in two *Super Bowl* games, I played in so many playoff games that it could have been its own NFL season, and I had the privilege of getting to hear from my childhood hero, Pete Carrol, on a daily basis.

The thing about any type of change we try to implement into our lives is that we usually look at things right up close, instead of the 30,000 foot view. This close-up viewpoint makes our confidence volatile because we all make mistakes.

We can have a tendency to not follow-through on being the people we want to be because of those mistakes...and no follow-through is all because of your viewpoint. If I would have given in to my close-up viewpoint, I never would have played for the *Seattle Seahawks* because I would have quit before I received that phone call. But you have to see things with the right viewpoint and this book, *The Boomerang Effect*, will help you do that.

I'm so proud of Malachi and how he has practically broken down this timeless principle: *What you sow, you will reap.* He has put this principle into actionable steps that can help anyone...and I mean ANYONE, get back up when they get knocked down. This book is one that each of us wishes we had as a young person. I know that if you will apply the principle how Malachi creatively teaches, the "Boomerang-Effect" will serve you well throughout your life.

Clint Gresham

THE BOOMERANG EFFECT

INTRODUCTION

If you throw a boomerang, will it come back to you? Not if you don't know what you are doing.

Many people do not know what they are doing when they "throw" things. And so they fail. And they give up. And they quit. And they cry. Stop crying, there's hope—all you have to do is learn *how* to throw!

LEARN! If you use the *wrong* type of boomerang, it will not come back to you—you need a "returning boomerang." So you need the *right tool*—not just a boomerang but a *returning* boomerang.

If you have the right boomerang but use the wrong throwing technique, it will not come back either—so that means you need the *right tool* and the *right skills.*

Now, if you have the right tool plus the right skills, does that mean you will have a successful throw?

NO.

What else do you need?

Well, you have to actually CATCH the boomerang when it comes back to you.

If you get distracted, it will slap you upside the head! If you walk away and give up, it will still come back but someone else will catch your success.

WHY would you get distracted? Why would you Give Up?!

Because your Mindset is set *wrong*. Maybe you are lacking in the mental toughness department so you do not stay in the game when the game gets tough. Or, you might have the right tools and the right skills, but you keep getting the same old average results so you give up. The same old results mean you are hitting a glass ceiling.

Your head must hurt!

I am not just talking about a Boomerang here. I'm talking about *life*. About goals and impact. About business and success. I had a goal, but that meant NOTHING until I combined it with the right principle. I had to get the right tools, the right skills *and* the right Mindset to shatter the glass of what is normal for a "kid" and Level Up. To do this, I decided to use a principle to my advantage.

The definition of "principle" is: *a fundamental truth that serves as the foundation for a behavior.* So a principle is a truth that you should base your "behavior" on. Principles are always at work. The problem? If you are not using the principle to your advantage, you are at a DIS-advantage.

Do not be dissed.

Think about a farmer. The sun is going to rise, it's going to set. A farmer can sleep in while the sun has risen and shining on his farm. He can get up around 10:00 AM, have some coffee, read the paper and watch a little TV, then get to work around 11:00AM. Is he using the "principle" of sunrise and sunset to his advantage?

NO! That is just not smart. He will have less daylight to do things that require daylight. And all his farmer buddies will outsell him and outproduce him. Work the principles to your advantage!

Here is the principle I want to focus on:

Principle → *The Boomerang Effect*

I say it like this:

What you sow, you will reap. What you throw, you will keep.

#TheBoomerangEffect

The results you have right now are because of the choices you made yesterday, last week, last year…and so on. If you are *stuck*, not moving forward and not getting any better it's because you are still "sowing" choices that are helping you stay stuck. You have to break out of your rut!

You need a weapon to break through things that are keeping you stuck at your current level. Real weapons will not do it. You need the Weapon of Strategy—the right one. Locked, loaded and ready to work the Boomerang Effect principle in a way that will put points on your scoreboard and shatter the glass.

My strategy shatters glass.

The Strategy is this:

BOOMERANG MINDSET
+
CORRECT ACTION
=
GLASS SHATTERED

The Boomerang Mindset that you will read about in this book is a way of thinking that was created to work WITH principles, not against them. Principles are at work without you, so why fight them? Use them!

The right Mindset gives *more* power to your Action. It creates more momentum. It causes your Action to reap above-average results! The right Mindset will give you enough power and momentum to shatter the container.

Who wants to be contained? It gets very stuffy and smells bad in there. So pick up your Boomerang and let's break through to the next level!

Every time you take Action, you are taking action with a specific Mindset and Attitude. Not only are you doing or saying something, you are doing and saying it with a specific mindset and attitude. So every time you take Action, the Boomerang Effect happens. What is the Boomerang Effect? *What you sow, you will reap. What you throw, you will keep.* This is what it looks like in action:

1. CHOOSE the Boomerang = Choose the MINDSET
2. THROW the Boomerang = Sow the MINDSET
3. CATCH the Boomerang = Reap the MINDSET

What do you catch? It all depends on which Boomerang (which *Mindset*) you chose to use when you took Action on your goal.

Bummer if you used the wrong Mindset.

Here is an example: Let's say you choose to have a "GET-TO" Mindset instead of a "HAVE-TO" Mindset when you are taking action. The GET-TO Mindset will cause you to do the task better and faster, people around you will *like* being around you, and you will get a positive result. It is all because of how you THOUGHT. You performed with a GET-TO attitude instead of a whiny HAVE-TO attitude. No one wants to be around you if you have a HAVE-TO sour face attitude while you are mumbling and grumbling about what you are doing.

"Selah." (Translation of "Selah:" Pause and calmly think about *that!*)

You have heard the phrase, "Level Up!" I like to say "Shatter Up!" Why? Because to go to the next level, you must bust through what is containing you. Leveling up requires an action of "Shattering" in order to move you to the next level! Don't you think it's time for a move? I do. So pick up your boomerang.

GET READY FOR:

THE
BOOMERANG
EFFECT

I am Malachi Walker and I approve this message.

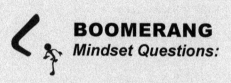

BOOMERANG
Mindset Questions:

1. Name one of your glass ceilings. Where are you stuck?

2. Think of a time when you used a *positive* mindset. What result did you get?

3. If one person does an Action while having a positive attitude and another person does the exact same Action, but has a negative attitude, will the result be the same? Why or why not?

#shatterup

GET-UP OR GIVE-UP?

CHAPTER 1

You might have stopped trying after your last fail. Why? It's because of your MINDSET. Now every time a new opportunity comes your way, your Mindset is set on GIVE-UP. So even if you choose to give it a try, it is just a *kind-of* try because you have already given up in your mind. That is a dangerous place to be!

Maybe most areas of your life are smooth sailing, but you might have *one* area that is always programmed on the GIVE-UP setting. When you hear about that area, the memories of your last experience rush into your mind—and they are not happy memories. Your palms get sweaty, your stomach starts feeling carsick and you quickly avoid any new opportunity in that area. What does this mean? You have given up.

Here is an example:

Maybe you had a horrible stage experience where you forgot your lines, or your voice cracked, or your legs and hands were shaking, or you stuttered through your speech, or you tripped and everyone laughed, or you ended but no one clapped, or the audience applauded but it was that awkward applause. The only thought you could think was, "If I ever get off this stage, I will *never* do this again!"

And you haven't. You stepped off stage and never tried again. You completely gave up. That is not a WIN! You are now trapped at the same level you were on when you were last on stage, whether you were eight or twenty-eight. Your glass ceiling will never be shattered in that area. And, you will *always* feel horrible about your ability to speak in front of an audience.

Who wants that defeated feeling to stay?! Defeat does not have a right to camp out in your mind—unless *you* let it.

GIVE-UP is what you are sowing so GIVE-UP results are what you are reaping. Unsuccessful and average results keep coming back to you because the principle is always at work. You will not even pick up a Boomerang and *really* try anymore. Forget about giving your best, how can you when you have already failed in your mind?

The *Boomerang Effect* is at work, but is it working *for* you or against you when you:

1. Keep CHOOSING the GIVE-UP Boomerang.

2. Keep THROWING the GIVE-UP Boomerang.

3. And it keeps RETURNING to you...and knocking you upside the head.

It's working *against* you! Your MINDSET keeps knocking you down and it will take some work to get back up. But you *can* get back up!

There are many ways you can get knocked down! You can get knocked down physically or you can get knocked down mentally… like when someone discourages you or when you fail at something you're trying to do.

So what do you do when you get knocked down?

YOU GET BACK UP!

It is that simple.

Getting knocked down is a setback. But, remember this success tip:

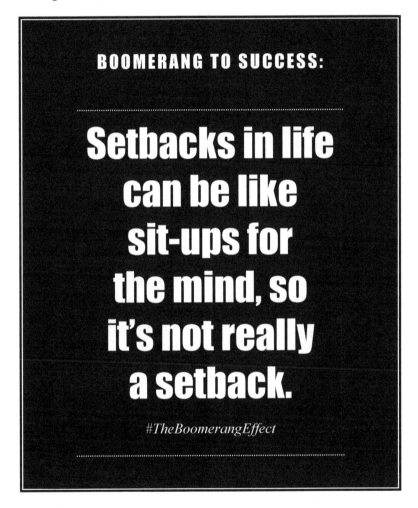

Every time you sit-up in your mind, your MINDSET gets stronger.

It is Mental Conditioning.

At the time, it may seem like a setback has moved you backwards (and it has). But if you learn from the setback and do a sit-up in your mind, that setback will boost you forward like you never knew it could.

It's a workout for your *mind muscles*. You do this by reaching for the GET-UP Boomerang when your discouraged mind really wants to reach for the GIVE-UP Boomerang. It takes work. Your MIND has to do a sit-up.

If you change your Mindset to GET-UP instead of GIVE-UP, it's going to come back to you and you will catch Success. That's the Boomerang Effect! You might not know when the Success will come back to you, but Get Up and throw again believing for successful results!

When you take action with a GET-UP mindset then your actions are more excellent, more brave, more focused and have more potential…all because you changed your attitude. But if you let that knock-down cause you to move forward with a GIVE-UP mindset, your actions won't be brave or focused, they will be fearful and half-baked.

I never liked half-baked food.

The sit-up happens when you CHOOSE the Mindset you will use to carry out the Action steps to reach your goal. It's hard work to push through how you feel and choose a different Mindset. No one likes sit-ups, but you do them because you like the

Remember, it is simple:
Choose It. Throw It.
Catch It.

1. **CHOOSE the right Mindset.**

2. **Take Action and THROW while *using* the right Mindset.**

3. **CATCH the returning Success that you created *because* of your Mindset.**

result. People do not always like getting back up and throwing again. But you will like the RESULT. So do the mental sit-up and choose the GET-UP Boomerang.

You *can* get back up from an injury, a bad business idea, a failed grade, a try-out that left you on the bench, parents who split up, a bad performance or from an embarrassing speech. Do the sit-up. Stop crying about it and Boost Forward! Throw the right Mindset!

BOOMERANG TO SUCCESS:

When a Setback happens, do a Sit-up in your mind. Choose the GET-UP Boomerang and not the GIVE-UP Boomerang. The new MINDSET will boost you forward farther than you fell back.

#TheBoomerangEffect

GIVE-UP
Boomerang

Boom!

 **GET-UP
Boomerang**

BOOMERANG MINDSET
SUCCESS STORY

When I was eleven, I was playing soccer, basketball, karate, and football. I was really into sports! I'd often win gold medals with my karate studio (The *Wheeler* Academy) at karate competitions, and my soccer team made it to the championship game many times— and won a few! I really enjoyed my life where I was. Then, my family had to move to Texas. From East Tennessee to Texas…and it was tough.

It was a quick move that none of us expected. Only four weeks from the day we knew we were moving, to the day we drove off in the moving truck. Crazy. I had to leave *The Wheeler Academy,* my soccer team, my church *(The Church At Knoxville)* and my friends, and I didn't want to. Texas and I were not off to a great start!

The one thought that kept me somewhat positive and hopeful was knowing there were some great soccer programs in the Dallas Metroplex area. I wanted to hit some tryouts, make a competitive team and get back to "normal" as fast as possible.

Finally, the spring rec season was wrapping up and there was only one week until summer. I could not wait! I was in the middle of soccer tryouts for an *FC Dallas* Select Team and was on the soccer field, playing a game. Off and on during the last season, my knee had been feeling strange. It would hurt for a bit, and then it would stop. Every now and then it would pop. After a while, I told my dad about my knee and he thought it was a little odd. He scheduled me an appointment with the Sports Medicine group at *Scottish Rite Hospital for Children.*

The morning of my appointment, I walked into the waiting area and I was rather optimistic. I was not expecting any big issue. Everyone was nice, the waiting room was chill and things were moving along like a normal appointment…until the doctor walked in to share the X-ray results.

My day changed real fast. He said I had a condition called Osteochondritis (OCD). There was not a specific moment or incident that caused the OCD. It was more of a growth issue. So the doctors decided that it would be best to rest my knee until we got an MRI to see it in more detail. The doctor encouraged me to stay positive and not jump to conclusions.

I was fine with that…rest a few days and then back at it! I was fine with the idea of rest *until* we got the MRI results and I found out how long I had to rest. Three months on crutches, then 6 months with a brace…then another MRI, and then 3 more months with a brace!

WHAT?!!

That was not what I expected to hear! I was not allowed to jump, run or do any sports for the summer and fall seasons. The doctor said if it did not heal in nine months, I might have to have surgery—then that would be 12 more months plus the 9 months!

THAT IS 21 MONTHS PEOPLE! A year and a half right when summer is starting. You are kidding me! My case of OCD was rather intense. If I wanted a chance at a normal knee that could play sports later, I had to deal with it now. So I was going to miss two summers, two seasons, two…you get the idea! And here I was in a new state, no sports team, no friends, and now no walking.

I hated the thought. Talk about a KNOCKDOWN! Talk about a SETBACK! I felt like someone threw me up against a wall, *BAM*, and I was sliding down the wall to the floor in a heap. All I wanted to do was just stay there, on that floor, feeling sorry for myself—for two years. I was reaching for the GIVE-UP Boomerang, ready to throw it and have it come back to me and knock me upside the head. The GIVE-UP mindset would result in two years of lazy living with average results.

NO!!

I thought about it and made a decision. I did the sit-up in my mind. At the time, I was a normal kid…school, sports, video games, church, and food. Being normal AND not being able to walk or play sports sounded crazy boring. My Aunt had told me about a guy named Caleb Maddix and I had been watching his videos. He had shattered the glass ceiling that kids and teens often hit. It is the same ceiling that contains many adults. Caleb did not let that happen! He is a motivational speaker, a business owner, a teenager and going after LIFE. Why couldn't I do the same?

I decided not to give a normal response to this setback. I hopped into the kitchen and told my mom, "I've been thinking about this. I'm bummed, I am. I'm mad too! But that doesn't fix anything. If I can't run, jump or work to be the best at sports right now, I've got to do something or I'm going to go crazy! I can't stand this. So I figured it out—I'm going to become a motivational speaker. I'll motivate while I wait."

I decided to CHOOSE a different Mindset to use during what looked like a one or two-year detour. So I let go of the GIVE-UP Boomerang and reached for the GET-UP Boomerang.

And I threw it!

Once I changed my GIVE-UP Mindset, the changes I was forced to accept because of my knee condition (like not walking) were easier to accept…a little easier. What I thought my next year was going to be had fallen through. Just stamp, "Failed Business Plan" on the front of that file.

But the Boomerang Effect works, even if you have to change your plan. What you put into something will return. I just had to change my skills, my techniques and my Mindset about the whole thing. Once I made the changes so I could use the Boomerang Effect to my advantage, I like what flew back to me!

Above-average results flew back! I'd wake up at 4:50 AM every day (thanks Caleb for the motivation!), do an hour workout, read my Bible and pray, record a YouTube video, edit the video, write this book you're reading right now, and then start school.

I did have to get some skills to do those things. I learned the beginning steps of how to record and edit videos and compose music for my vids, so that I could start a motivational YouTube channel. I came up with some new goals and kept working toward them. I hated the thought of *normal* results. Of *average* outcomes. I didn't want to sit around and wait. I couldn't be great at sports anymore, at least for a year—so I had to take that setback and do some major sit-ups.

Don't you hate the thought of getting *normal* and *average* results?

That whole time demanded SIT-UPS in my mind—it demanded focused Mental Work and it was hard! I had to fight against my failed "business plan" of making the top soccer team. There were times I wanted to throw that "I'll motivate while I wait!" statement out the window and into the trash. And every time I chose not to trash it, I chose the GET-UP Boomerang and did a SIT-UP in my mind.

The Boomerang Effect principle is always working. Whether it is a good result or a bad result, you *will* get a result. So you need the right Strategy in order to get a good result. When I sowed the GET-UP Mindset as I went to work towards my new goals, I reaped the GET-UP results! I liked the results.

Whatever Mindset you choose will come back to you.

The fact that you are holding my book in your hands right now proves that the Boomerang Effect principle works—and the GET-UP Mindset helped me shatter the glass ceiling that wanted to contain me.

The moral of the story is: No matter what knocks you down in life, Get Back Up! I could have moped around just playing video games and watching TV with no goals, no drive and a bunch of average results, but I didn't. I did not want to get average results. I wanted to stand out, and I still do want to stand out. Don't you?! So do something!

BOOMERANG TO SUCCESS:

....

Get Back Up and throw the Boomerang with passion again, no matter what is standing in your way.

#TheBoomerangEffect

....

HOW TO GET BACK UP

A lot of times you will want to quit. But when you choose not to quit, and choose the GET-UP Mindset, you become stronger in your mind...you just did a mental Sit-up! If your mind is strong, you will get through many hard things in life that you thought you could not get through. You will not survive hard times if you do not choose the GET-UP Mindset. It is too easy to GIVE-UP and let things stay the way they are.

And sit at the same level day after day, stuck under that same glass ceiling.

If you really want to get back up, you have to do that *yourself.* The only person who can choose a GET-UP Mindset is *you.* What will you choose? If you choose to sow defeat and take action with a GIVE-UP mindset, you will reap a GIVE-UP half-baked result.

That strategy will not shatter any glass.

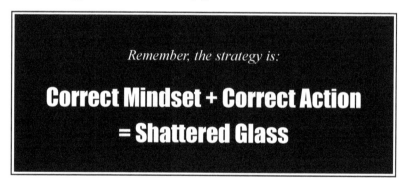

Remember, the strategy is:

Correct Mindset + Correct Action = Shattered Glass

It might be a hard choice to throw the GET-UP Boomerang because you won't *feel* like it after a failed result. But if you make the right choice, then you are using the Boomerang Effect principle to your advantage! You will reap success if you do not quit or give up!

The doctors at *Scottish Rite* were nice and encouraging, but I still had to go home and deal with the results that they found. I felt alone. I felt empty at times. Frustrated. Angry. But even if you feel all alone, remember that you have a secret weapon. Your weapon is the Boomerang Effect—it's the principle that is always working. It will be on your side if you will use it right! You are never alone—the principle has your back!

As I faced that huge unexpected slap in the face, I prayed a lot and read my Bible. "What you sow, you will reap," is in there (in Galatians 6:7) and when I connected that principle to the Boomerang picture, I felt inspired again. Invigorated again. Like there was a plan that I could use to make this huge disappointment worth something.

There was a way to deal with this loooonggg rest and actually make some good tasting lemonade out of the sour lemons.

I'm sure many who will read my book have your own stories of injuries and disappointments. What I dealt with might seem like a walk in the park to a lot of people. We all have different things we face, but please know that the Boomerang Effect will work for you, no matter what you are facing!

You can probably think of one area in your life right now where you are choosing GIVE-UP. You might still be trying but you are not *really* trying. Just going through the motions. Your work or school might be great but your home life might be failing. Are you going to choose to stay knocked down? Sitting there and doing NOTHING to move anything forward? Like having an injury and choosing to mope about it for two years?!

Or, are you going to choose to get back up and do EVERYTHING you can to move forward? Like having an injury, but still choosing to do whatever it takes to create new goals, a new vision and a new plan and then go after them!

Are you going to stay knocked down and keep throwing with a GIVE-UP mindset or are you going to do the sit-up and throw with a GET-UP mindset?!

It depends on whether you want to Shatter-Up and break through your glass ceiling, or stay contained and just sit there.

It's time for *you* to choose! Personally, I say,

SHATTER-UP!!

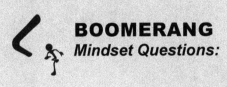

BOOMERANG
Mindset Questions:

1. Name something in your life that you are doing, but you know you are just going through the motions. (For example: school, work, family, church, workouts, etc.)

2. Why are you satisfied with going through the motions and getting average results?

3. Name one action you can take with a GET-UP mindset to get better results.

#shatterup

BOOMERANG SUCCESS MINDSET

CHAPTER 2

You want to Shatter the glass ceiling, right?

You want to accomplish a Goal, right?

You want to become Successful, right?

Have you ever thought that there is a right way to *think* if you are trying to accomplish a goal or to be successful? Well there is and I'm going to tell you.

As we talked about in Chapter 1, the Boomerang Effect is happening all the time! Whether the effect is GOOD or BAD depends on what you are throwing. *What you sow, you will reap. What you throw, you will keep.* If you believe it or if you don't, it's still a principle no one can escape. You can run, but you cannot hide. Kind of like gravity. Just because you don't believe in gravity, it does not change the fact that if you step off an airplane, you are going to fall fast.

And when you hit the ground, it will not be a glass ceiling that shatters!

The right Boomerang is a weapon that will help you. The wrong Boomerang is a weapon that will hurt you. Whether you choose the right Boomerang or the wrong Boomerang, it will fly out of your hands, affect those who are in its path, and then fly back straight to YOU.

In order to choose the right Boomerang, you have to have the right way of thinking. I call it the:

BOOMERANG SUCCESS MINDSET

I figured it out by looking at one of the main differences between BABIES, KIDS and ADULTS. It's how they think about their goals. All three age groups combine together to create the Boomerang Success Mindset, so let's take a look!

FIRST → BABIES:

Well, babies don't really have major goals in life, like kids and adults would define a goal. But babies still have goals. Their goals are to get what they want, to get what they need and to have fun… period. That is their Mindset. They are throwing the Boomerang of I WANT-I NEED-HAVE FUN and that is what comes back to them! They get their Wants, they get their Needs, and they have Fun.

SECOND → KIDS:

I understand this way of thinking well. Most kids think of a goal like this: "I want to be this…I want to do that…When I grow up, I'm going to be a…." Most kids think like that about a goal. We are really good at DREAMING a goal and BELIEVING we will achieve that goal—no matter how big it is! It's our Mindset. I've heard the saying, "The faith of a child can move a mountain." But a Dream needs Action if it's going to accomplish something. It's like a math equation.

Dream + Action = Move the Mountain

So kids DREAM their goal and have FAITH they will reach their goal one day, but most kids do not know what to do to accomplish their big goal. Their Mindset is DREAM BIG and HAVE FAITH, so Dreams and Faith come back to them. More dreams! More goals and more ideas, because that's all they are throwing. But if that's all you throw, that is all you will reap…and you never have anything that becomes "real."

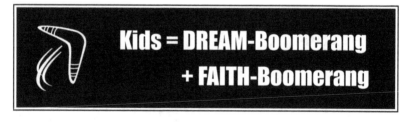

Kids = DREAM-Boomerang + FAITH-Boomerang

That's why there are a lot of kids who have grown up to become adults and they've never become their "When I grow up, I want to be…" dream. Because kids grow up and then one day realize that they did not become or reach that goal. Why? Because they didn't add enough action to their dream.

When you are a kid, you need someone (usually an adult) who knows what it will take to make your DREAM happen and who will help you along the way. Kids are good at throwing out Dreams and Faith, but then WHAT?!

I have two coaches, I call them "Boomerang Coaches," who told me these things. Boomerang Coaches are coaches who know how to train others on the *Boomerang Success Mindset*. They know what it takes to make a dream happen and they don't fluff it up just cause I'm young.

One thing my Boomerang Coaches did not do was teach me how to throw an actual boomerang. Maybe I can ask Logan Broadbent, member of the First Place USA *Boomerang 2016 World Cup Championship Team* for that coaching! (Hint…hint…if Mr. Logan is reading my book.)

Why do so few adults tell youth how to take action on their BIG goals? If you are an adult, you should help at least one youth look at their big goal with the right equation in mind. Dream + Action = Success. You don't have to be a full-time *Boomerang Coach*, but at least do something. Tell a youth these Boomerang Success Steps and get them this book!

As you consider how kids think about goals, ask yourself:

1. Am I *doing* the work that it takes to accomplish my dream?

2. Am I talking about my dream but not doing anything about it?

Which one are you? How about you say it AND do it?!

Kids are very confident in their goals. They think they can do or be anything. Some actually do it…most don't.

THIRD→ADULTS:

How do adults think about goals? Well, it's very simple. I can describe it with one word: COFFEE!

Just kidding, just kidding.

Ok, back to business.

Most adults think like this about a big goal: "It will take lots of time. I need more money. It will take more connections. I have too much other stuff to do. It's too late. I'll just keep doing what I'm doing."

You know what I mean?

Adults *know* it takes time and lots of work to accomplish a goal. They are real. Unlike the way kids or babies thinks, an adult thinks immediately about all the WORK a goal will take. They throw the WORK-Boomerang…a lot. Too much sometimes.

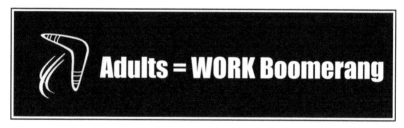

Some adults use their knowledge as a reason to call their goal impossible—which is really an excuse, not a reason. But some adults use their knowledge that a goal takes lots of Work as an advantage.

You ask how?

I shall tell you.

An adult can use the knowledge that a goal is going to take a lot of WORK as an advantage because that knowledge turns their goal from impossible to POSSIBLE. Why? Because they know what it takes to make that goal happen. They are not just dreaming about it, they are *doing* something about it. They make the choice to have a Work Mindset and then they throw the WORK-Boomerang.

Knowing what it takes to make something happen makes it possible! Adults also use time management to get things done. They tell their mind that it is going to take a lot of work—and then they do the work!

Some will do all the work that's needed to accomplish the goal.

But most will only do part of the work and then give up, which is very easy to do.

To Review:

#1 Baby Thinking: FUN-Boomerang

#2 Kid Thinking: DREAM-Boomerang + FAITH-Boomerang

#3 Adult Thinking: WORK-Boomerang

Which of those three MINDSETS do you use the most?

Which type do you think you *should* use the most so that you can make your goal happen?

DRUM ROLL...

Out of #1, #2, and #3, the successful way to think is...#4!

BOOMERANG TO SUCCESS:

....

Combine the good things from Adult-Thinking, Kid-Thinking, and Baby-Thinking to create Boomerang Success Thinking!

#TheBoomerangEffect

....

To Shatter-Up you need all three.

Ok, ok, I'm sorry for ruining your chances of getting the question right! You couldn't get it right because I didn't give you #4 as an option. Just keeping you on your toes! But really, #4 is the right way to think if you are trying to become successful and make your dreams happen.

#4 is a MINDSET that is a mixture of #1, #2 and #3. See, all generations need each other! Let's hold hands and sing! I'm kidding. But, we can definitely work together.

From #1 BABY THINKING, #4 takes the Baby's main goal: HAVE FUN.

 If you are trying to accomplish a goal or become successful, have fun with it! Whatever your goal is, it needs to be something you enjoy because you're going to be spending A LOT of time on it. So have fun while you are doing it! Throw the FUN-Boomerang and you will have FUN as you work! This way you won't get bored or burn out.

From #2 KID THINKING, #4 takes the Kid's main goal: DREAM BIG + HAVE FAITH.

If you are trying to set and accomplish a goal, do what kids do. Dream big and have Faith! Keep your major goal BIG and believe you can do it!! Throw the DREAM + FAITH Boomerangs so you won't be easily discouraged or become stagnant.

From #3 ADULT THINKING, #4 takes the Adult's main goal: WORK.

Know what it takes to become successful! But do not let that discourage you. Just make sure to do the work to become successful. Break it down into steps and do the steps. Throw the WORK-Boomerang.

Take the best from #1, #2 and #3 and you have created the:

#4 = BOOMERANG SUCCESS MINDSET

I want you to remember the #4 way of thinking and what it takes from numbers 1, 2 and 3 so you can Shatter your glass ceiling!

A Thought on Why Adults Give Up

I think many adults start their big goals but don't reach them because they:

1. Stop having FUN
2. Lose the big picture of the DREAM
3. Stop having FAITH that it can actually happen

Once these three things happen, there is nothing to fuel all the work that a goal requires. Soon, they stop. If you are only throwing the WORK-Boomerang, then that's all that comes back to you. Work, work, work. How boring is that?!

You need to throw the FUN-Boomerang more…and the DREAM-Boomerang more…add some FAITH-Boomerangs off and on and *then* you'll be throwing the WORK-Boomerang with the right Mindset so that your "car" doesn't run out of "gas."

Stopped being bored.

If you are an adult, you need to think like a kid sometimes. And kids need to think like adults sometimes. That's why we can make a great Team! Remember, the *right* strategy will shatter your glass ceiling. The right strategy is to use the Boomerang Effect to your advantage. You now know the principle: *What you sow, you will reap. What you throw, you will keep.* So as you are trying to level up, be sure to throw FUN, DREAM, FAITH and WORK-Boomerangs so that what comes back to you is a finished goal and a Shattered ceiling!

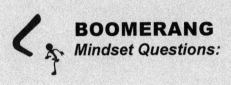

BOOMERANG
Mindset Questions:

Choose one of your goals and ask yourself:

1. Am I having FUN as I work towards this goal? If so, How? If not, Why?

2. Do I really BELIEVE I can accomplish this goal? If so, How? If not, Why?

3. What WORK have I done to reach this goal?

4. What three main steps are necessary to reach this goal? Am I working on each step?

#shatterup

BOOMERANG MINDSET TEAMS

CHAPTER 3

You do not have to feel happy to throw the Boomerang of POSITIVITY. Feelings will lie to you and tell you that you have to act how you feel. But you don't have to act how you feel. When something goes wrong, think of what went right. When you are sad, choose to look happy. When you lose, have the attitude and character you would have if you just won. Be positive and it will come back to you! People will want to be positive back and you will actually feel better.

What you sow, you will reap. What you throw, you will keep. You always have a choice about how you are going to act. A bad result does not give you permission to act all Negative!

Stop that!

At the *Boomerang World Cup*, there are different types of events. There are team events and individual events. The Boomerang Effect principle has teams too. They are Mindset Teams. There are only two teams and they are exact opposites: Team POSITIVITY vs. Team NEGATIVITY. There is always a Positive way to look at something—no matter what. And the opposite is true. There is also always a Negative way to look at something.

So it's simple. The principle is at work and the game is ON! Which team are you playing for?

Team POSITIVITY

vs.

Team NEGATIVITY

Once you choose your team, it will be easier to reach for the right Mindset at the right time. It's like settling on your favorite brand of tennis shoes for a particular sport. When you need a new pair of shoes, you go right to that brand and pick a pair of shoes from that brand. There's no need to search the store for other brands because you've already made up your mind about which brand of shoe gives you the best results for your sport!

BOOMERANG TO SUCCESS:

....

Make up your mind that being Positive will always give you the best result.

#TheBoomerangEffect

....

Once you make up your mind that being Positive will give you the best results, it will be easier to choose the right Mindset. It's like setting one of those remote control cars on a track. First you choose which track to set the car on, then all that's left to do is push "go" and the car goes in that direction.

Reach for Smile instead of Frown. Reach for Get-To instead of Have-To. Reach for Peace instead of Worry.

If you are a Boomerang Success *Thinker*, then you already know which Team to join.

| Team Positivity:
Choose It.
Throw It.
Catch It.
It is that simple. | Team Negativity:
Choose It.
Throw It.
Catch It.
It is that simple. |

I like listening to and reading books by successful people. As you think about which Mindset Team to join, take a look at two lists I put together from reading "Positive Dog" by Jon Gordon (best-selling author and keynote speaker).

What Team POSITIVITY will bring your way:

THE BENEFITS OF BEING POSITIVE

(Unless otherwise states, quotes are from "Positive Dog" by Jon Gordon)

1. Positive people live longer. In a study of nuns, those who regularly expressed positive emotions lived an average of 10 years longer than those who didn't. (Snowdon, 2001)

2. Positive work environments outperform negative work environments. (Goleman, 2011)

3. Positive, optimistic salespeople sell more than pessimistic salespeople. (Selifman, 2006)

4. Positive leaders are able to make better decisions under pressure. (Institute of HeartMath, 2012)

5. Positive people who regularly express positive emotions are more resilient when facing stress, challenges, and adversity. (Jon Morgan)

Set your mind on the right thought-track, this way your thoughts will go in the right direction.

#TheBoomerangEffect

6. Positive people are able to maintain a broader perspective and see the big picture, which helps them identify solutions; whereas, negative people maintain a narrower perspective and tend to focus on problems. (Fredrickson, 2009)

7. Thankfulness cancels out stress. You can't be thankful and stressed at the same time. (Malachi Walker, 2017).

8. Positive emotions, such as gratitude and appreciation, help athletes perform at a higher level. (Institute of HeartMath, 2012).

9. Positive people have more friends, which is a key factor to happiness and longevity (Putnam, 2000).

10. Positive leaders are more likely to be supported, make good decisions, receive pay raises, promotions, and achieve greater success.

Look at everything Team Positivity will return back to you! So make the choice to be a Positive Thinker—*that* is the Boomerang Success Mindset. It's all in the mind, so do the Mental Sit-up when you are about to say or think Negative and CHOOSE to say or think Positive instead.

Why? Well, what does the opposite of a Positive Mindset get you? You can probably take a wild guess and get the answer right. But just in case, here are a few results of choosing Team Negativity. Enjoy the read.

THE COST OF NEGATIVITY

(Unless otherwise stated, quotes are from "Positive Dog" by Jon Gordon.)

1. 90% of doctor visits are stress related. *(Centers for Disease Control and Prevention)*

2. A study found that negative employees can scare off every customer they speak with—for good. (Rath, 2004)

3. At work, too many negative interactions (compared to positive interactions) can decrease the productivity of a team, according to Barbra Fredrickson's research at the *University of Michigan.*

4. Negativity affects the morale, performance, and productivity of our teams.

5. One negative person on a team can create a miserable environment for everyone on the team.

6. Robert Cross's research at the *University of Virginia* demonstrates that 90% of anxiety at work is created by 5% of one's network—the people who sap energy.

7. Negative emotions are associated with decreased life span longevity.

8. Negative emotions increase the risk of heart attack and stroke.

9. Negativity is associated with greater stress, less energy, and more pain.

10. Negative people have fewer friends, because people do not like being around negative people. (Malachi Walker)

These tips are plain good reasons why choosing your Team should be a No-Brainer. Team Positivity is a BOOMERANG SUCCESS TEAM. Join it because success will come back to you if you are on this team.

Having a Positive Mindset has a lot to do with helping you become Successful because you don't get all focused in on the Negative parts. It helps you to see the BIG picture of what you are in the middle of.

You need to see the Big picture or you will stay Small.

BOOMERANG TO SUCCESS:

Decide to be a POSITIVE PERSON and it will help you see the big picture. Your life will change for the better..

#TheBoomerangEffect

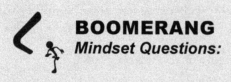

BOOMERANG
Mindset Questions:

1. Of the ten "Benefits of Being Positive" listed in this chapter, what are your favorite two?

2. Of the ten "Cost of Negativity" listed in this chapter, which one can you relate to?

3. List the three people (other than family) that you are around the most (i.e. sports team members, friends, business partners, etc.). Label them as being on Team-Positivity or Team-Negativity.

4. If any of them are on Team-Negativity, what are you going to do about that?

5. Look at question #3, how would those same people label you?

#shatterup

WHICH TEAM ARE YOU THROWING FOR?

CHAPTER 4

Deciding to be on Team POSITIVITY is the smart choice and gives you a head start. But, you *still* have to choose to pick up a Positive Boomerang instead of a Negative Boomerang every time you react or take Action. So here are two examples of the Boomerang opposites to give you an idea of how it works.

I've learned that I don't *have* to do things, I *get* to do things. If I have to wash the dishes, it's a lot easier if I choose to be thankful that I have dishes and I'm not eating off the floor. So I tell myself, "I *get* to wash dishes." And that's not always easy to do and I don't always do it right away. I'm growing.

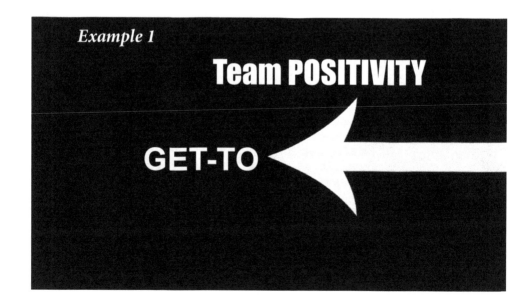

If you have two Boomerangs at your fingertips, ready to throw, which one would you choose? One of them has "HAVE-TO" written on it and the other one has "GET-TO" written on it. Let's say you really dislike the task you are about to do so your emotions are all ticked off. It would be natural to grab the "HAVE-TO" Boomerang and hurl it as hard as you can!

There is one problem with that though. That same Boomerang is going to fly back at you, with the same attitude you threw it with. When it comes back and smacks you in the head, you will be even more agitated! And, you *still* need to finish the task. Your bad attitude has changed NOTHING except to agitate you more. I know because the HAVE-TO Boomerang has about knocked me out several times!

The HAVE-TO boomerang NEVER works in your favor. It just makes the HAVE-TO task harder to complete and a lot less enjoyable for *everyone* who HAS to be around you while you are doing it. Stop acting like that!

I believe you can.

Even though the HAVE-TO Mindset often appears "strong and forceful" because you are agitated, it's not the right kind of strength

Change the words "HAVE TO" into "GET TO."

✔ HAVE-TO

✖ GET-TO.

#TheBoomerangEffect

and force to boost you forward. It actually keeps you trapped because it flies back to you as an Action completed but with an attitude all jacked up. It's kind of like purposefully making a bunch of loud noise with the dishes while you have-to wash them. You will not be shattering any glass ceilings with that Mindset!

Do not pick up the wrong Boomerang. If you do, you can't respond right. Choose to use the *Boomerang Success Mindset* and stay on Team Positivity! You have a choice. So pick up the GET-TO Boomerang and throw it! Shatter yourself out of the HAVE-TO mindset!

There is a thankfulness feeling that goes with the GET-TO Boomerang. It helps you to be thankful for the task, even though you don't like it. If you can see the end of the task and stay calm enough to remember the result you will get once you finish the task, it will make the task easier to do.

Like this: If I wash these dishes, I'll have clean dishes the next time I want to eat…and the kitchen won't smell.

Stop letting your emotions work against you. Pick up the right Boomerang and stay on the right Mindset Team!!

LIFE IS A GIFT, ACT LIKE IT

Everyone can put a positive perspective in front of any situation. Here is an extreme example to show us we have no excuse to whine around: I've known someone dying a painful death and he still managed to put a positive perspective in front of that situation. My great-grandad would say, "At least I'm alive at this moment and I got to live this long." He passed away in peace because of his perspective.

Thinking about that situation makes the HAVE-TO attitude about washing the dishes seem very lame.

Sometimes it takes something horrible happening to someone before they realize that they need, or needed to be, more positive. Sometimes it takes feeling lots of pain before someone realizes that they should not have complained so much about their life, because it was a gift. Some people don't choose a positive perspective or realize how great their life was until they suffer pain or loss.

That sounds horrible, doesn't it? Complaining so much that you do not realize *that* life is a gift. Do you really want to be that kind of person—a complainer?! You will be throwing for Team Negativity your WHOLE life and you will be around NEGATIVE people all the time.

You shouldn't want to live like that.

Put a positive perspective in front of everything you see in life. Realize how blessed you are! Life is a gift, so enjoy it because you only get one chance to live it. Choose the right Mindset and remember what team you are on. Don't you dare touch the HAVE-TO Boomerang...put it down...walk away.

Stop being frustrated and realize you are blessed! You are blessed enough to have this book, you are blessed enough to be alive and have a roof over your head. If you are not living in a house, at least you're blessed enough to still be living.

Since you are a *Boomerang Success Thinker*, you have a *Boomerang Success Mindset*. That means you are throwing for Team POSITIVITY. But it doesn't mean you will just automatically be positive all the time. Positivity is a choice you have to make.

So when you feel Frustrated, you have a choice between two Boomerangs. One Boomerang has FRUSTRATED written on it and one has BLESSED written on it. The Boomerang you choose to throw will fly back to you and you will catch it or it will smack you down! You will catch the BLESSED attitude, but the FRUSTRATED attitude will fly back and smack you down because frustrated attitudes always work against you.

Example 2

Team POSITIVITY

BLESSED

....

The Boomerang will fly back to you with the same attitude you threw it with.

#TheBoomerangEffect

....

So does Team Negativity. Frustrated attitudes cause you to speak, act and treat others with irritation. No one likes that! It will just grow and irritate you and those around you. And you won't accomplish much anyway because no one works as good or as fast when their attitude is all jacked up. You also make more mistakes because you are blinded by your attitude. You might be taking Action towards your goal, but you could be doing it with the wrong Mindset. The

Boomerang Effect principle is at work and returns that Frustration right on back to you.

You might complete an Action, but who have you ticked off while you were doing it? What if they were part of the next step you needed and *you* drove them away? Remember the Strategy that will shatter your glass ceiling?

When you feel Frustrated, remind yourself which team you are on. Remind yourself that the result will be worth it. That you do not have to listen and obey your emotions. YOU are a *Boomerang Success Thinker* on Team POSITIVTY. When you are Frustrated, choose to pick up the BLESSED Boomerang *anyway!* Isn't it amazing—the difference between success and failure is often simply your attitude.

Boomerang Mindset + Correct Action = Glass Shattered

BOOMERANG MINDSET
SUCCESS STORY

When my family moved to Texas, we stayed in a small apartment while we waited on our house in Tennessee to sale. It was less than a third of the size of the house we moved from. We didn't think we'd be there long, but it got longer and longer and longer! Well, the kitchen was small, actually it was TINY. 6 ft. X 3 ft. of floor space. Imagine my brother, two sisters, my mom, dad and me in that kitchen at meal times or trying to get ready before we raced out the door in the morning. There was enough space for a stove, a dishwasher, a sink, a fridge...and a person (that's singular: "A" person).

There were times when it was FRUSTRATING, especially trying to get to the dishwasher or fridge without wanting to knock someone over who was in the way. So, it was very easy to think things like this: "MAN! This kitchen is way too small, get out of my way, stop bumping into me. I can't do *anything* in this kitchen!" Yes, I did say that a few times and, yes, my mom gave me that look she gives.

We didn't even have a real kitchen table because the eating area had to double as an office for my mom's business. So we would take the folding table out when it was time to eat and then put it away when the space had to turn back to an office. All six of us would squeeze around that small folding table for a meal. My parents called it family bonding time and I called it family FRUSTRATION Time. But you know what? Our family grew strong.

The situation went from a three-month lease to a two-year lease. It wasn't anyone's plan. Our family had to choose the BLESSED-Boomerang. Complaining wasn't an option—even if we were FRUSTRATED. Can you imagine six FRUSTRATED-Boomerangs flying around that place?! Talk about Team Negativity.

My parents have always been big about our family being a team. If one of us "score" a point, it's a point for the whole team. If one of us are having a tough time at something, we all feel it and should do something to help, either by praying, encouraging, or working. Why? "...because it affects the whole team!"

BOOMERANG TO SUCCESS:

....

Complaining should never be an option in your mind.

#TheBoomerangEffect

....

Now, that is the beautiful picture of "family" in my parents' mind, but you know we don't always act that way. It's a goal. We are a Boomerang Mindset *Team*. Our minds should all be set in the same direction for the Team.

Your family should be a Team too! And on your Team, should you allow Negativity? No! Don't be constantly ducking because of the zinging NEGATIVE-Boomerangs flying around your house? If you're having a Negative attitude, you are helping your Family Team lose. Maybe you've never thought of that. If not, you should.

You should think about it now.

In fact, get your family members this book, each of you read a chapter a week, and then go through the *Mindset Success Questions* (that are at the end of each chapter) on Sunday as a Team. Do something different as a family so you can get a different result! And if the kids don't like it, well just do what my parents do and make us. In the end, it will turn out good.

The Boomerang Mindset Team idea works for a lot of things in your life. Like business. Your company should be a Boomerang Mindset *Team!* So, what is flying around your office? Are the employees throwing a bunch of HAVE-TO and FRUSTRATED-Boomerangs?

If so, your company is Team-Negativity and when you compete against a company that is Team-Positivity, your company will get beat! Why? The Boomerang Effect. *What your company sows, it will reap. What your company throws, it will keep.* You just read the list of ten results you will get when you are Negative, right? So your company will lose.

I'm not being mean, I'm just being real. Maybe you need to get your employees this book and have some Mindset Strategy sessions for how your business can become a Boomerang *Mindset* Business that is throwing for Team Positivity! If you want me to come speak to your business, let me know. You might need to do something different to get a different result. Having a teenager come in for a Mindset Strategy session could be the difference you need so your business can Shatter-Up!

OK, back to my story.

Complaining in that tiny space was contagious, like a cold, and it killed the atmosphere. Nobody wanted to be around anybody when NEGATIVITY-Boomerangs were being thrown, but there was nowhere to go to "get away." So we had to find a good way to look at where we were or we'd hate life for two years. Why do that?

And, I was on crutches and in a bulky brace—which just *added* to a FRUSTRATED feeling and shrunk that tiny kitchen even smaller. In fact, the narrow hallway I had to go through to get to the bathroom, and to the room I shared with my brother, was barely wide enough for my crutches. Once I did take that enjoyable, clumsy hallway stroll to my room, I had to hop around on one leg because there were so many moving boxes stacked along the wall that using crutches was more of a hazard than a help.

Really?!

Remember, not only was the apartment tiny, we had packed out a house three times the size within four weeks so the three-month apartment idea was also serving as a quick storage unit. I could go on and on, but I'll stop…because I need to throw the BLESSED-Boomerang now before I become Frustrated at the memory.

The Walker Family had to survive mentally. So, as best as we could, we tried to pick up the BLESSED-Boomerang to throw when we were Frustrated. If all of us were committed to be on Team Positivity, we at least had a chance of survival. Six BLESSED-Boomerangs flying around the tiny apartment actually made it fun—at times. (I'm not gonna lie, it wasn't always fun.) None of us always chose the right Boomerang. But we tried. When some were having a weak moment and picked up a FRUSTRATED-Boomerang, at least someone else would try to choose the BLESSED-Boomerang, so it still helped.

For example:

When I was aggravated with the crowded eating experience, I had to choose to say or think the right thing. "This kitchen is obviously NOT a dream kitchen, but at least I have a kitchen that is stocked with food and I'm not stranded outside having to survive by hunting my food and cooking it over a fire. I'm blessed to have this kitchen. And…I'm blessed that I can at least still get around, even if that means using crutches." Seems simple, but it really did help me.

You should try it too.

The Positive Mindset is the Boomerang Success Mindset. *What you sow, you will reap. What you throw, you will keep.* Since my family tried hard to throw POSITIVE-Boomerangs during those LONG two years, we had a lot of Positives come back to us. Now, we are in a home and all of our Mindsets are stronger because of that tiny apartment. We are a stronger Team. My sisters, brother and I all have our own rooms and the kitchen in the new home is nothing like that tiny apartment. I sure do appreciate it more and I know I'm blessed.

Throwing for Team-POSITIVITY is *always* the right throw and it's part of the Strategy that will shatter your glass ceiling. My family shattered the glass ceiling because of the Mindset we developed from that experience. It was either that or actually be shattering glass as we threw plates at each other out of Frustration. You just have to choose what you want the most.

And then go get it.

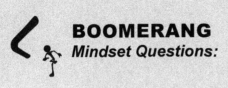

BOOMERANG
Mindset Questions:

1. What task, job, chore, assignment or exercise will you change from HAVE-TO to GET-TO?

2. List three things you usually Complain about. Now, say something Positive about each of them.

3. What did you learn from the Mindset Success Story about Malachi's tiny apartment experience?

4. Name your top Frustration. How can you label it as a Blessing?

#shatterup

X-USE THE EXCUSE

CHAPTER 5

The word "Excuse" tries to trick you because it has the word USE in it.

Do not be tricked.

If you have ever made an excuse about something, you've USED an excuse. So you have likely been tricked by the word. Everyone has. Excuses may not seem like they are a big deal, but they are a very, very big deal.

Excuses can become a habit. A habit is something you do over and over, and you often don't even know you are doing it. The EXCUSE habit will weaken your Mindset and cause you to put a lot of points on Team Negativity's scoreboard. *You* cannot do that! You are a Boomerang Mindset Thinker.

Drop the EXCUSE-Boomerang. Back away. Slowly, slowly, slowly….

PUT AN X ON IT

To remind myself what the word Excuse really means, I spell it like this: "X-Use," meaning, "don't use." I put an X on it! Cross it out! No Trespassing! Do not take one more step closer to that EXCUSE-Boomerang!

There will ALWAYS be a logical reason to reach for the EXCUSE-Boomerang. For example, when a student does not want to be honest and just say that he forgot to do his homework, you might hear this famous Excuse: "The dog ate my homework."

It's usually logical to use an Excuse (though "the dog ate my homework" is not that logical.) Excuses get you out of trouble and help make the truth not hurt so much…at least when you *first* use them.

But then they fly back.

The Boomerang Effect hurts when what flies back to you are the consequences of an Excuse. *What you sow, you will reap. What you throw, you will keep.* There are a lot of grown up people who have EXCUSE-Boomerangs flying back to them because of a situation where they used an Excuse instead of the truth. Those returning Boomerangs are causing a lot of trouble for their careers, their health, their families, their finances and more!

Be a person of character. Throw the right Boomerang when people are watching and when they are not. And please stop using Excuses! Excuses like, "The dog ate my homework" sound even more ridiculous coming out of an adult's mouth.

You know, if you are a youth reading this don't think that you can use Excuses now and when you are an adult, you'll just automatically stop. That's not going to work! Adults have the same habits they had as a youth unless they have chosen to change them. So do the work now and create the right habit. X-out the Excuse!

Excuses give you permission to choose GIVE-UP instead of GET-UP, to choose HAVE-TO instead of GET-TO and to choose FRUSTRATED instead of BLESSED. Which means, when you use an Excuse you are throwing for Team Negativity.

These Boomerangs are spelled differently, though it's the same word. Why? Because when you make a choice to either *use* an Excuse or *not use* an Excuse, then you have chosen your mindset and the Boomerang Effect begins! Remember: Choose It. Throw it. Catch It.

If you choose to not use an Excuse, then you are picking up the X-Use Boomerang and you *will* get a positive return! You have put an X on the Excuse and have chosen not to go near it—that is what Boomerang Mindset Thinkers do!

Boom!

Team NEGATIVITY

 EXCUSE

On the flip side of the coin, if you choose to use an Excuse, then you will get a negative return. Why? Because you chose the *wrong* Mindset and have empowered the Excuse. I hope you enjoy your view through that glass ceiling.

Do not throw for the wrong team! It is easy to reach for an EXCUSE-Boomerang and want to throw it. Excuses are easy! But you will get a Negative result because an Excuse causes you to *not* try, to *not* do your best, and to *not* believe the best. When you use an Excuse, you are throwing for Team Negativity.

Don't do that.

Put an X on the Excuse and do not use it. When you do this, you are being honest with yourself and with others. "The dog ate my homework" is not being honest and that Excuse does not create a potential solution. "I'm sorry. I procrastinated and didn't get my homework done. Is there any way I could do it for partial credit?" Great! Now you have opened the door for a potential solution to return to you.

The truth can hurt, but the truth is real. When you choose the truth, then you can stare the problem in the face and look for a potential solution. If you are using an Excuse, you are not dealing with the truth. You're living in lah-lah land. Put an X on the Excuse. Do not use it!

DO THE DRILLS

Let's say that you are at practice and the team is running drills. You haven't done anything wrong, but the coach still tells *you* to run two extra suicides. What should your Boomerang Mindset Response be?

You do the two extra drills. And you do them with excellence.

Do not make an Excuse to try to get out of it. Do not try to excuse yourself from becoming better! Don't complain and say, "But *they* aren't doing two more!" If they did two more drills like you, is that changing how many *you* do?

No, of course not! Then why are you trying to make up an Excuse for why you should not have to do it? Excuses will reap average results. If you have to do more drills than everyone else does, WHO CARES?! You are getting better than them!

No Excuse! Each time you choose to put an X on the Excuse that comes to your mind, you are becoming a stronger Boomerang Success Thinker. So whether you are on the court or field running drills, or dressed in a suit and sitting in a skyscraper tall business office, do not make Excuses.

Do the drills.

BOOMERANG TO SUCCESS:

....

Every time you use an Excuse, you weaken your own mind. Put an X on the Excuse and get your strong mind back!

#TheBoomerangEffect

....

WHY DO YOU CHOOSE THE EXCUSE?

If you want to be the best, you obviously cannot be a person who is getting average results. If you are fine with average results then you're never going to accomplish BIG things. Knowing WHY you use Excuses can help you X them out.

Sometimes the Excuse is there because you don't want to do the Work, or you don't think you *can* succeed, or you feel something isn't fair. That's how I felt at first when I found out about my knee. There were a lot of logical Excuses for me to use to excuse a bad attitude or bad work ethic. But I had to choose to put an X on those Excuses and turn them in X-Uses!

I did not need a bunch of Negative EXCUSE-Boomerangs flying back at me. What result would I get from that? The result would be to empower me to have a *bad* attitude and a *lazy* work ethic for a year! And then, that bad habit would be created and who knows if I would have ever broken out of it.

NO! I needed the X-Use Boomerang flying back at me with potential *solutions* to my problem of a year without being able to walk normally. Writing this book and getting it published are two of the solutions that flew back at me when I chose not to throw the EXCUSE-Boomerang.

It is Boomerang Mindset Conditioning. Tell yourself to GET-UP and throw POSITIVITY. Remind your Mind that the Work will accomplish something great and X-Out the Excuse!

BOOMERANG MINDSET
SUCCESS STORY

I was fasting. My church youth group, *Legendary,* was taking part in a church-wide fast that *Covenant Church* was also doing. I was giving up desserts for 40 days. Not easy, but I wanted RESULTS. One Sunday we came home from church and my parents told us we were going to be having some guests over that night for a Super Bowl party. I didn't really think much about it, until it was party time and the kitchen island was filled with Super Bowl Party food… which included my favorite…DESSERTS. Really good-looking desserts. Mouth-watering desserts. And. I. Wanted. Some.

The struggle was real people. I couldn't even enjoy watching the game. The desserts blinded me. I battled it in my mind a while and then I made a very logical decision. "Mom, I didn't think about the Super Bowl being during this fast. I'm just going to have some dessert and then restart my fast tomorrow. It really isn't a big deal. I mean, it's the Super Bowl, it only happens once a year!" This sounded completely logical to me. LOGICAL.

Sometimes you need other Boomerang Mindset Thinkers to bounce your "logical" ideas off of. She looked at me, with that expression, and I just knew she wasn't buying my Excuse. "I know this is hard! But think about *why* you started your fast. You have some goals and results you want. You can break the fast today and restart it tomorrow, but what if you lose out on a result? The dessert will taste good now, in this moment, and then it is over. But the results *you* are after will last Malachi. You make the choice, just be sure your choice gets you the results that you want the most."

Thanks mom.

I'm thirteen, can't you give me a break?! I guess that's an Excuse

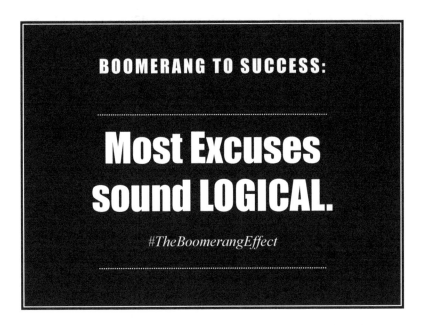

BOOMERANG TO SUCCESS:

Most Excuses sound LOGICAL.

#TheBoomerangEffect

isn't it? Age should not be an Excuse! My mom was handing me an "X" to put on my "But-it's-the-Super-Bowl-Excuse." It was *my* choice to take that X and use it. Which Boomerang was I going to throw? The EXCUSE-Boomerang would be the easy throw. But in my gut, I knew it would not return to me with the result I wanted. I knew I'd regret it as soon as I finished eating that tasty dessert. The PAIN of choosing to put an X on the Excuse and throw the X-Use Boomerang is real! It is Mindset Conditioning! It makes you stronger!

So I did what I'm telling you to do. I chose the X-Use Boomerang. What helped me do that? I chose to put my focus on what was going to fly back to me. I'd either get a tasty treat for a few minutes, or I'd get a result that could influence my entire life...all based on which Boomerang I chose to pick up.

"Delayed gratification" they call it. It's worth it in the end.

A couple of the results from that fast that flew back to me after my Super Bowl decision was that I met the CEO of *Beyond Publishing* and the company partnered with me to publish my book! Also, former NFL Seattle Seahawk Clint Gresham agreed to write the Foreword for my book—which is a big honor! I don't understand all of the hows and whys behind spiritual fasting but I believe the fast made a difference in those breakthroughs. Can you imagine if I would have forfeited my publisher and an NFL Super Bowl winning football star for a piece of chocolate cake and a logical Excuse?!

Stand firm.

COMMON EXCUSES

Here are a few common Excuses that my Boomerang Coaches and I have thought about:

1. The "I Can't" Excuse

An Excuse is easily used when you are not *willing* to do what it will take to make something happen. In that type of situation, you can do it but you are not willing to. Do not make up a bunch of lame reasons for why you "can't" do it (lame reasons are called Excuses). Just say what's true. "I don't want to." When you say you can't, you usually mean you don't want to. If you wanted to bad enough you could likely figure out a way.

And don't say you will do it, when you know in your heart that you will not put in the work to finish it. Because then you will just have to make up a bunch of Excuses for why you "can't" finish it. Be honest from the beginning—say, "I'm sorry, I just don't want to." You see, it's not "I *can't*," it's "I don't *want* to."

At least that is a fact and not a lie. Then you are also telling *yourself* the truth too. Don't lie to yourself. Excuses help you lie to yourself. When you lie, you are throwing for Team Negativity. It might sound good, but it comes back to you bad because lies are always brought to the Light and the Truth is seen.

Protect your character and just be honest. Say, "Thanks for asking, but I don't want to be involved." I've seen my parents have to do this a lot. They have taught me the difference between "I Can't" and "I Don't Want To." I have to keep practicing it, but at least I understand the difference.

2. *The "I Don't Have To" Excuse*

Excuses will tell *you* to skip steps. Excuses will tell *you* to take the elevator to success. Excuses give your mind a reason for why *you* should not have to do something...even when you see your teammates, friends, family members or business partners doing it. That is not right! Take the steps and put in the work. Excuses will tell you to take shortcuts, so do not listen to them. Put an X on them and call them an X-Use! Do not use them.

3. *The "I Don't Have Time To" Excuse*

Not having enough time is true *sometimes*. But most people use time as an Excuse. Just think of all the small things you don't do because of "no time." Cleaning up the kitchen, driving your car through a carwash, making your bed, returning a call, sending an email and things like that. People check their Insta accounts or are on Social Media so many added up minutes in one day that "no time" for those small things is usually an Excuse! Really—you could not send a text message response because you had "no time?!" X that out!

And make your bed. Everyone has time to make his or her bed.

TV, Video Games, Social Media...these are time stealers and people still use the Excuse of, "I didn't have time to." See, that is usually a lie. When you pick up a Lie and throw it, the Lie flies back to your Mind and you actually believe it is true. Then you end up excusing yourself from doing something you *could have* and *should have* done. You *do* have time to make a phone call, to respond to a text or to give someone a five-minute conversation.

No Excuses. Stop that!

BOOMERANG TO SUCCESS:

Excuses help you lie to yourself. Then you are living a lie and you think it is true.

#TheBoomerangEffect

GET RID OF EXCUSES

Honestly, I still make Excuses. But at least I'm committed to putting an X on them and turning them into an X-Use! I must keep on doing Mindset Conditioning so I will not get lazy and start using Excuses. Excuses are *easy* to use! It's so much easier to reach for an EXCUSE-Boomerang, isn't it? But your Mindset gets weaker with each Excuse. My sister is a gymnast and she doesn't always do each gymnastics skill perfectly, but she is committed to constantly getting better and she shows up in that gym six days a week.

You should be committed too.

Excuses make you look bad, Excuses make you look less smart, less intelligent, less positive, and look like a bad leader. Excuses are bad for business, bad for your team, bad for your brand and bad for your reputation. Here are a few Negative Results that fly back to you when you choose to throw an EXCUSE-Boomerang:

EXCUSE DISADVANTAGES

1. **Excuses get you average results.**

2. **The more Excuses you make, the longer it will take to succeed.**

3. **Excuses make you sound unprofessional.**

4. **People see through your Excuses.**

5. **Leaders who make Excuses for problems will be beat by leaders who are Problem Solvers.**

There are so many other ways that Excuses make you look bad. I'm not going to go through those because that would take a very, very long time.

Instead, let's get to work putting an X on the Excuses with some Mindset Conditioning!

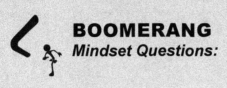

BOOMERANG
Mindset Questions:

1. Name two ways that Excuses help you lie to yourself.

2. Think of someone who often makes Excuses. Why is it hard to trust them?

3. Will Excuses make it easier or harder to reach your goals?

4. Name one Excuse you often use that sounds *logical*. Do you feel you should stop using that Excuse (X-Use it)?

#shatterup

MINDSET CONDITIONING: STEPS-TO-SUCCESS

CHAPTER 6

My sister, Lyric, is a gymnast at *Texas Dreams Gymnastics.* It's a world-famous gym filled with athletes who are constantly trying to Shatter-Up! Chris and Kim Zmeskal-Burdette (First American to ever win the Gold All-Around at *Worlds* and Olympic Bronze Medalist) own the gym. *They* know the importance of conditioning!

Lyric starts every day, but Sunday, in the gym at 7:00 A.M. with a five-hour practice...no big deal. (I am joking.) The first hour is Conditioning. An HOUR of conditioning, *before* they start training their events...you can stop complaining about your 20 minute jog now.

Conditioning is part of any training. Your *mind* is no different. You are not just born thinking like a Boomerang Success Thinker. You have to go through Conditioning to *become* a Boomerang Success Thinker and to stay a Boomerang Success Thinker. Training your Mindset to think the best is going to take work! Remember, how are you going to shatter the glass ceiling that is trapping you in? By having the right Mindset. And to do that, you must Condition.

Physical Work + Mind Work = BOOMERANG SUCCESS

"The only way to become successful is to work." When people say that, they usually mean physical work. But that is just *part* of what you need to do to become successful. The other part of the work must be done *in your mind.*

BOOMERANG TO SUCCESS:

....

Mindset Conditioning will make your physical work easier and more productive.

#TheBoomerangEffect

....

When it's super hard to choose a Positive Boomerang but you do it anyway, you are *conditioning* your Mind. Yeah, it's hard but it becomes easier to choose a Positive Boomerang the next time. Yeah, it will hurt and you might get "sore." But just like my sister (who seems to be sore ALL the time) when that soreness wears off, you have stronger muscles. Remember, being a Boomerang Success Thinker on Team POSITIVITY is not automatic. It is a MINDSET choice. And name me a Sports Team that does not condition!

Many of the things I'm asking you to do in this book may be challenging, but in the end it will be worth it! There were times I wanted to pick up a Negative Boomerang and knock someone out with it in that tiny apartment (no offense if you are reading this book). But every time I would choose a Positive Boomerang instead, my Mindset got stronger. I got "sore" some. It felt like my mind was running suicide drills. But that is how you GROW! And in the end, it helped me because the Boomerang Effect is a fact: *What you sow, you will reap. What you throw, you will keep.*

Let's do some Mindset Conditioning!

If you put in the work, on-purpose, to make yourself think a certain way then your Mindset will grow stronger. Those things that irritate you will become less and less. They might not change, but since you have changed which Boomerang you pick up when irritating things happen, you are now the one who has power over those irritating things! That's called Shattering-Up! That's called Conditioning.

I've broken the Mindset Conditioning down into five STEPS TO SUCCESS. Stop taking the elevator instead of the Steps. Get your game-face on—it is time to CONDITION!

MINDSET CONDITIONING

Step-To-Success #1:

COMMITMENT

Everyone has a goal—some people just do not call it that. The people who say they don't have a goal *could* have a goal, but they will not do the work to accomplish that goal so they usually will not call it a goal. Maybe they call it a dream. An idea. A vision. A one-day-I-want-to.... so it is not a goal because there is no commitment. It's just a thought. But, it only takes a strong decision to turn it into a goal!

That decision is to throw a COMMIT-Boomerang! Boomerang Success Thinkers condition their mindsets to look at a dream or an idea differently. Tell yourself, "I changed my Idea to a Goal and I will not stop until my Goal is accomplished!" You might have to tell yourself that a lot. That is called Mindset Conditioning.

Just do it.

Do you see the difference in what your Mind has to do? You must Commit to changing the way you see a dream or an idea. Most people only think of their dream unrealistically and so their dream will never come true. When you make a choice to Commit, you are throwing the COMMIT-Boomerang and it will come back to you as a goal accomplished! That is what a "dream come true" is. Dreams do not just happen, they take commitment. To *stay* committed you have to condition your Mindset.

COMMIT is Mental Conditioning Step #1 because it is a choice and choices happen in your Mind. If you remember to keep throwing for Team POSITIVITY while you stay committed, it will make it easier.

The Boomerang Effect, Malachi Walker | 95

BOOMERANG TO SUCCESS:

Some of the hardest work you will ever do is in your mind.

#TheBoomerangEffect

BOOMERANG MINDSET
SUCCESS STORY

In Chapter 1 I told you about my knee condition. I used to be so mad about it. I wanted to throw my crutches up against the wall hundreds of times. It screwed up my goals. But I couldn't live thinking like that. I wanted to blame everything, even God. My knee forced me into Mental Conditioning. I couldn't just sit around getting all bitter and out of shape!

Once I "dreamed" some new dreams and came up with new ideas, I turned them into goals. I could have left them as ideas…and you wouldn't be reading this book right now. To make that shift from idea to goal, I had to Commit.

In the last ten months that I've had to deal with my knee condition and wear this brace, I've accomplished more than I would have if I didn't have the injury. It was all because I chose to Commit to the goal of not wasting the year. What were some of the results? I wrote this book you're reading, started and manage a YouTube channel and Facebook page, recorded regular Facebook Live motivational videos, I was featured in a coding app, and I was one of fifteen people chosen out of 3.8 million people in a coding contest…this is in addition to accomplishing other day-to-day goals.

How did I do it? Mindset Conditioning.

First, I stopped feeling sorry for myself. Second, I took an idea, and threw the COMMIT-Boomerang so that it turned into a goal. I chose not to let an injury push my new goals off track or slow them down. I committed myself to the work it takes to accomplish a goal. I knew there would be obstacles to get to my goal, and there were, but I chose to stay Committed and I had positive people around me encouraging me to keep my commitment.

It was tough at times and I didn't always have the best attitude. But I tried hard to treat those Obstacles as Opportunities! I told myself, "I've committed to turn my idea into a goal and to do the work my goal requires!"

I didn't know it, but each time I picked up the right Boomerang and threw it, I was becoming more of a Boomerang Success Thinker.

It was Mental Conditioning and wasn't easy! Some of the hardest work you'll ever do is in your mind. *What you sow, you will reap. What you throw, you will keep.* When you throw the COMMIT-Boomerang, Success will fly back to you!

Facing the fact that an idea takes Commitment to make it a real goal helped me wake up to real life. No goal is easy, if it was it would not be a goal. Ideas are easy but goals are not. When you make a goal EXPECT that it will demand your Commitment. It will yell at you like a coach, "Don't call me a Goal if you're going to wimp out and not Commit!!"

BOOMERANG TO SUCCESS:

Ideas are easy, but goals are not. Goals demand Commitment.

#TheBoomerangEffect

If you do not want to commit, don't make the goal. Be real with yourself. When I haven't accomplished a goal, it was because I didn't Commit to it. I wasn't real with myself about what it would take to make that goal happen, so it just stayed an idea.

When you COMMIT, you are using the Boomerang Success Mindset. Every time you choose to *stay* Committed, you are doing Mental Conditioning. Now, it's your turn! What idea can you turn into a goal by making the *choice* to throw the COMMIT-Boomerang?

MINDSET CONDITIONING

Step-To-Success #2:

PERSEVERANCE

A lot of people who know what their goal is and have Committed to that goal do not use Perseverance, so they fail. Here is the definition of Perseverance—*steadfastness in doing something despite difficulty or delay in achieving success.*

This means pushing towards success and choosing not to give up when delays or hard times come. When you are reaching for success, or just living life, there is going to be failure. There are going to be delays and hurdles you have to jump over.

Stop being surprised by that.

Just jump the hurdle and keep running! Remember, you have Committed. Now you have to Persevere. When you choose to jump the hurdle and keep going, you are picking up the PERSEVERE-Boomerang and throwing it. It will come back to you as a hurdle successfully jumped!

Life isn't just like a simple fun little princess game, where everything is perfect and easy and blah-blah-blah. That's not how life is. Life is tough; life is rough. But you can get past those tough times—by doing the Mental Conditioning and picking up the PERSEVERE-Boomerang. Aren't *you* on Team POSITIVITY? You can jump over those hurdles if you choose to Persevere.

Do not give up; keep pushing towards your goal! Learn from those

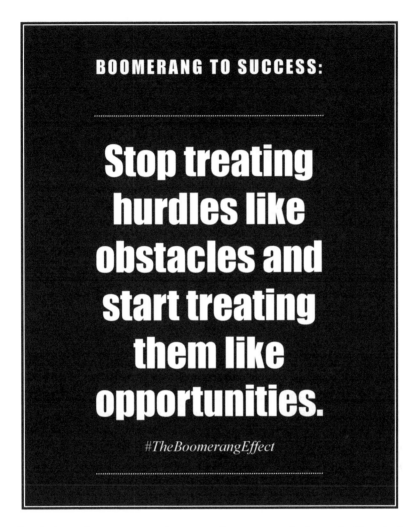

BOOMERANG TO SUCCESS:

Stop treating hurdles like obstacles and start treating them like opportunities.

#TheBoomerangEffect

hard times in your past that you chose to push through. Remind yourself of the times you have seen the PERSEVERE-Boomerang come back to you as an accomplishment! Persevering is a choice and then your actions will match your choice. So do the MIND WORK and it will BOOMERANG back to you…not as a dream that is still in lah-lah land but as a Goal that's been *Scored!*

MINDSET CONDITIONING

Step-To-Success #3:

CONSISTENCY

We have hit two of the Steps-to-Success Boomerangs that you will use as you are working towards your goal:

> (#1) COMMIT-Boomerang

> (#2) PERSEVERE-Boomerang

The third Step-to-Success is what holds COMMITMENT and PERSEVERANCE together. It is CONSISTENCY.

So you have to use the Boomerang called CONSISTENT. It will keep flying back to you as checkmarks in those little goal boxes. If you have Committed to your goal and you are Persevering towards your goal, you need to *Consistently* choose to *keep* Committing and to *keep* Persevering.

Some people work towards their major goal only once a week; don't do that! Consistently work towards your goal, or success will not come back to you. Throw the CONSISTENT-Boomerang once a day!

This conditioning step is like one of those automatic baseball machines that shoot balls at the hitter. It consistently shoots a ball. Over and over. There's a rhythm and the hitter expects the ball to come. Why can't you be Consistent like that with the work you need to do to make your goal come true?

BOOMERANG TO SUCCESS:

....

That one chunk of work that some people do once a week needs to be done every day. Be consistent!

#TheBoomerangEffect

....

Consistent people get more things done; and if they are working towards their goal, they will get their Steps-to-Success done faster than the people who are not Consistent. There are many people who have the same goal you do, and are trying to *beat* you to that goal. If you are more Consistent than they are, you will accomplish the Steps-to-Success faster; and the faster you get these Steps accomplished, the faster you will reach your goal! These are Mindset steps, but they create the right action that will accomplish your goal and Shatter your ceiling!

That makes perfect sense.

Consistency means "taking action regularly," but in order for you to do that, you must win the Mind Battle and *stay* Consistent. When you want to sit on your couch, watch TV and eat chips, it is Mental Conditioning to GET-UP and choose to throw the CONSISTENT-Boomerang again so you can keep your Commitment to Persevere and finish your goal. Being Consistent does not mean you don't relax *some*. You need to recharge—but not *every* night, for hours on the couch, in front of a TV. GET-UP people!

You also need to be using the Boomerang Success Mindset by remembering to throw the Have-Fun + Dream Big + Faith Boomerangs as you Work! These help you stay Consistent when you're about to let down your guard and allow Distraction to creep up to the door…and seep in…and join you on the couch in front of the TV…for three hours.

Think of the Boomerang Effect when you want to sit on that couch: *What you sow, you will reap. What you throw, you will keep.*

So are you going to do the Mental Conditioning or sit there and eat chips?! Get-Up!

MINDSET CONDITIONING

Step-To-Success #4:

FOCUS

Both of my sisters have trained in dance as part of their gymnastics training. My older sister is the gymnast and my younger sister was a gymnast but she decided to transition to soccer and track. Lyric and Maya have told me that when they are doing their "turns" in dance, they have to "spot." They pick a spot to focus on so when they turn, they quickly shift their heads and grab that spot with their eyes. It helps them not get dizzy and keep good form. Where am I going with this?

Your "spot" is your main goal. As you are spinning through your day, remember to "spot" your goal. It will keep you grounded and focused. It will keep you inspired. You will be able to handle the dizzy spinning of life if you can keep your goal in your vision.

When you notice things are getting fuzzy, uninspired, dizzy and boring, then an alarm should go off and shout, "Get your Focus back!!" This is an important Step-To-Success, so you must pick up a FOCUS-Boomerang and throw. Regain your "spot."

"See Spot run."

That's right. Stay focused on Spot.

There will be many things trying to distract you from your goal. The steps that it takes to accomplish your goal will break if you stay on one too long. So keep on climbing! If you get distracted, you will be stuck on a step too long because you are doing a million other

Your goal is right in front of you. But when you spin in a circle, 99% of what you see is not your goal; only 1% of what you see is your goal. Focus on your GOAL!

#TheBoomerangEffect

things. That step can "break" if you're on it too long. You might get burnt out, lose inspiration or even forget what your goal was, and on and on. When that step breaks, you fall and have to start all over to regain your Commitment, Perseverance and Consistency *again*.

That's not called leveling-up, that's called leveling-down.

So Focus on your goal and you will not get distracted, fall and have to start over. It's easy to get distracted from your goal when you see all of the other stuff happening around you. But ask yourself, "In the end, what is most important?" The spot is!

Stick with the plan and take the Steps-to-Success. You can do it if you really want to. You are a Boomerang Mindset Thinker, you're *tough* and you don't want to be contained!!

Throw the FOCUS-Boomerang!

BOOMERANG TO SUCCESS:

There are many steps to get to the prize that is way up there. Stay focused.

#TheBoomerangEffect

MINDSET CONDITIONING

Step-To-Success #5:

BELIEVE

"Believe" literally means the same thing as "Faith." If you do not have *faith* that you can accomplish your goal, then you have *fear* that you *will* not accomplish it. But if you don't try, you will fail. So faith and fear both have something in common, they are both thinking about the future.

Your mind gets stronger every time you choose BELIEF instead of FEAR. The future has not come yet, stop being afraid! You will either Believe that you will accomplish your goal, or you will have Fear that you will fail your goal.

"I believe in my goal!" It might be hard at times but *choose* to pick up the BELIEF-Boomerang! Why not? Do the conditioning so that choosing to Believe becomes your habit. Do not believe you will just *reach* the ceiling, Believe that you will shatter it and keep going!

Which statement is better for you to use? *I believe I CAN be the best.* Or, *I believe I WILL be the best.*

Hmmm…CAN or WILL?

When you Believe you *can,* it opens the door for Fear and Excuses. CAN means: "being able to." Well, what if you get started and you figure out that you really are not able to do that thing you need to be able to do in order to reach your goal?

You can throw BELIEF-Boomerangs all day, but until you get the skill you need to do what you have to do, you actually *cannot* do it. That is not a reason to pick up a FEAR-Boomerang! Instead, do not have Faith that you *can,* have Faith that you WILL.

If you Believe you WILL, then you won't create this Excuse: "Well, it's a fact that I simply *can't* do that. So I guess I should get a different goal." No, believe that you WILL and say, "It's a fact that I can't do that right now, but I believe I WILL do it because I will choose to learn the skill I need so that I CAN do it."

Do not say, "I believe I *can* accomplish my goal." Say, "I believe I *will* accomplish my goal!" Do not say, "I believe I *can* become successful." Say, "I believe I *will* become successful."

Throw the BELIEF-Boomerang, but Believe you *will* accomplish your goal not that you *can* accomplish it. That takes Mindset Conditioning! Set your mind to Believe! When you Believe that you WILL, you put an X on all the Excuses and turn them into X-Uses.

Boomerang Mindset Thinkers do not use Excuses; they turn them into X-Uses and then go get the job done! Go ahead and say this aloud: "I believe I WILL accomplish my goal! I don't believe I *can,* I believe I WILL!"

That feels different, doesn't it? You should say that many times each day.

STAY IN THE GAME

The Steps-to-Success demand a strong mind. But do not get discouraged if you feel like your mind and willpower are not strong. Any time you set a goal and then use even one of the Steps-to-Success, you have become stronger because the Boomerang Effect works! What you sow, you will reap. What you throw, you will keep. So each time you become stronger in your mind, you are closer to Shattering-Up the next time.

So stay in the game! Here are the Steps-to-Success at a glance:

THE BOOMERANG STEPS-TO-SUCCESS

Step-to-Success #5:
BELIEF → Throw the BELIEF-Boomerang!

Step-to-Success #4:
FOCUS → Throw the FOCUS-Boomerang!

Step-to-Success #3:
CONSISTENCY → Throw the CONSISTENT-Boomerang!

Step-to-Success #2:
PERSEVERANCE → Throw the PERSEVERE-Boomerang!

Step-to-Success #1:
COMMITMENT → Throw the COMMIT-Boomerang!

TheBoomerangEffect:

What you sow, you will reap.
What you throw, you will keep.

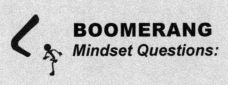

BOOMERANG
Mindset Questions:

1. List the five Boomerang Steps-to-Success. Then, circle the Step that is hardest for you.

2. Why is that Step-to-Success hard for you?

3. What good result will you get if you condition your mind to do that hard Step-To-Success?

#shatterup

BOOM!

CHAPTER 7

The purpose of this book is to help you Shatter your glass ceiling. It's to help you go to the next level—to "Shatter-Up!" It's to help you do what I did and break out of an unexpected experience. My book is to help you to *not* let unexpected things contain you or tell you who you are.

The choice to train my mind on *how* to think was the biggest factor that kept me from being trapped by a glass ceiling. Yes, I did a lot of actual work to write the book and reinvent myself, but all of that was because I pressed through and changed my mind.

The Boomerang Effect principle was already there, it has been around since the beginning of time, but it took me conditioning my mind so that I could use the principle to my advantage. When I conditioned my mind, I was able to explode out of the wrong way of thinking about my injury and create a new way of thinking.

I call this

BOOM!

Conditioning

The right way of thinking is to choose the right Boomerang and to stay positive. It is still a daily choice. But just like working out, once you create the right habits you just need to *keep* doing them and you will *keep* getting good results. The hardest part is breaking the bad habit and creating the new one. That's why you need the *BOOM!* in your conditioning, because you have to bust out of that "thing" that is containing you and *explode* to the next level!

The victory is in your MIND! Win the battle in your mind and you will be able to Shatter your glass ceiling. You know that there is not really a physical ceiling, so it's not your physical strength that will get you to the next level. This is true for athletes too. Yes, you need physical conditioning, but if your mindset isn't also conditioned—you will get beat.

Mindset Conditioning is important! So here are some Mindset Conditioning Exercises to help you work out your mind and break some bad mental habits. It's *BOOM*-Conditioning! Come on, pick up the right Boomerang and let's get to work!

BOOM CONDITIONING!

Exercise #1:
X-USE EXCUSE CHART

Do this for one week. Keep a tally each day of how many Excuses you make. Keep it simple, enter it in your notes on your phone—just type Monday and then if you make an Excuse, enter an "X." At the end of the day, count the X's.

For example: Monday→X X X X X X X X = 8 Excuses.

You can write it on a napkin if you need to, just do it! The Mindset Conditioning comes in here: The next day, keep on marking your Excuses but intentionally choose to make *fewer* Excuses. When you see yourself getting close to the number of Excuses you made on the first day, FIGHT to *not* make another one that day! Come on, WIN!

Beat your score every day and your Excuse habit will be exploded—*BOOM!*

For example: Tuesday →X X X X X X X = 7 Excuses.

Great, you turned one Excuse into an X-Use! Your mind is already getting stronger because it takes a mental decision not to make an Excuse. Tomorrow, X out another Excuse!

EXCUSE-Boomerangs do not just appear, they are created by your habit of *using* them. If you are not trying your best at *not* making Excuses, you won't just make the *same* amount of Excuses—you will start to make *more!*

And that's not cool.

Every time you throw an Excuse, it comes right back to you and lays at your feet ready for the next time you "need" one. We usually do not realize it when we make Excuses, but if you will focus on *not* making them, you will quickly realize the Excuses you make. Then you can decrease them!

This is *BOOM*-Conditioning because the habit that might be keeping you trapped at your current level could be the Excuses you always make. You could have all the answers and steps right in front of you, but you won't do them because of your pattern and habit of making Excuses. Use this exercise to help you explode and demolish that bad habit.

Don't you want to hear *your* ceiling shattering?! Come on,

BOOM CONDITIONING!

Exercise #2:
THROW TWO BLESSED-BOOMERANGS!

Everyone is blessed with someone or something. Stop and throw two BLESSED-Boomerangs right now! Name two of your blessings right now and THROW!! Do you feel that? It comes back to you like a baseball caught in a glove—*Whoosh,* it just feels GOOD!

Conditioning your Mindset to see the Positive and not the Negative will help you speak and act Positive more often. But sometimes you have to do it on-purpose. That is why I said to "Stop and throw two BLESSED-Boomerangs right now!" (If you did not do it the first time I wrote it, I just gave you another chance.)

You can do this as many times as you want each day! Every time you choose to label a blessing, you are doing Mindset Conditioning and you are getting stronger. As you get stronger, you begin a habit of reaching for POSITIVE-Boomerangs. And if it's a Negative attitude and mindset that is containing you, then creating this Positive attitude habit could be the last step you need to *explode* out of the container that is holding you.

BOOM!

I know it sounds simple, but most people are soooo close to leveling up. Negativity kills chances of Shattering-Up. What if the only thing left for you to do was to start speaking and thinking Positive? Do the *BOOM*-Conditioning exercise. Retrain your mind!

Come on, isn't it time you are the one who hears the *BOOM?!!*

BOOM CONDITIONING!

Exercise #3:
NEGATIVE vs. POSITIVE!

If you are a Boomerang Success Thinker, you have to stop throwing COMPLAINT-Boomerangs. Complaints are always Negative AND it sounds like you are whining...come on, you're not 4.

Make a simple list of how many times you complain today. Then you will realize how much you complain.

Tomorrow, try to decrease your Complaint Score. How? Complaints are NEGATIVE-Boomerangs so you need to throw POSITIVE-Boomerangs instead. Do this by saying the opposite of the complaint that comes to your mind. When you do, your Positive Score just went up and your Complaint Score did not. It will not be easy because you won't FEEL like being Positive. That's why this is Mindset CONDITIONING.

Do the sit-up.

Make it a CONTEST. Do this each day until your Complaint Score is 0 and your Positive Score is at least 50. Your Positive score is unlimited, so do not limit yourself to exactly 50 Positives every day. Try to increase your Positive Score and keep your Negative Score at 0. This won't happen overnight, but do not give up!

You are after the *BOOM!* You deserve to hear your ceiling Shatter too!

You know, when you do this you will find yourself feeling a lot happier with life. There are so many people who take medicine because they are so depressed. Maybe they don't need medicine to not be depressed. Maybe they just need to do this exercise until they actually hit 50 positives a day and it becomes their new normal. Depression swims in Negativity, but Positivity drives away Negativity. Just a thought. Make a chart and be proud of each Positive mark!

My family had to do this in that tiny apartment. We did not actually make a chart, but I'm sure if my mom would have thought about it she would have headed straight to the store to buy one of those big pieces of neon colored poster board and keep track of the contest... you know how moms can be. But if you think making yourself a chart will help, then do it. Do what it takes!

Press through towards this goal, do not give up! This is *BOOM*-Conditioning! Stop giving up when you start something. Start the contest and make sure you hear the *BOOM!*

BOOM CONDITIONING!

Exercise #4:
TEXT A THANK YOU

Send a short text to someone and THANK them for something. Thankfulness is always a Team POSITIVITY Boomerang. Do this ONE time each day. Set a reminder on your phone. Call it Positivity Conditioning. Schedule it, like you schedule a meeting.

Seems simple, doesn't it? You'll be surprised how easy it will be to *not* complete this exercise. So many people are thankful for something someone else has done or said, but they never throw the THANK YOU-Boomerang. Do not be that kind of person. It's one text/day. Throw it! It's called Conditioning and *you* are a Boomerang Success Thinker. Send the text, you will like what you catch!

Sometimes people are trapped by their bad ability to recognize what others have done for them. Telling people "thank-you" not only creates a better relationship, it does something inside of your mind and heart. This could be the mindset change you need in order to hear the *BOOM!* Do the exercise and become a person who recognizes others and actually lets them know it. It will change *you!*

It might change you right on up to the next level…Shatter-Up!

USE THE RIGHT MINDSET
WHEN YOU ARE CONDITIONING:

Boomerang Success Thinkers use the right Mindset when they are conditioning because conditioning is hard work. Remember Chapter 2's way of thinking? Have FUN with what you are doing + Keep your DREAM in front of you + Have FAITH that even if it's hard you can do it + Do the WORK. Think this way and the conditioning will be easier!

Do not give up, even when challenges come or when life gets hard. It's crazy to think that picking up the right Boomerang is hard, but you know that's true! That is why I call it *BOOM*-Conditioning. Choosing the right attitude, which is the right way of thinking, can feel like you are trying to move a mountain. It's hard because attitude and mindset start *everything* in motion, so you are not just changing your attitude and mindset, you are changing the whole flow of your mind-traffic.

Who knows, these exercises could be that last bit of tweaking that you need to help you Shatter your glass ceiling! Come on, pick one and let's throw. Explode that mountain right on out of the way— *BOOM!*

Mindset Conditioning is not easy. But easy things do not shatter glass.

#TheBoomerangEffect

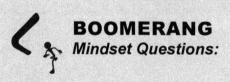

BOOMERANG
Mindset Questions:

1. Of the four BOOM-Conditioning Exercises, which one will help you the most?

2. Why will it help you?

3. Which exercise will you start today?

4. Let's check one off right now. Pick up your phone and send a Thank You Text. (And do not get distracted by your notifications—you are stronger than that!) "Send the Text and you'll like what you catch."

#shatterup

SAVAGE NOT AVERAGE

CHAPTER 8

Have you ever had a result that you just hated and you knew the bad result was your *own* fault? I'm sure everyone has. This happened to me the other day. The reality of a choice I made months ago flew back to me and stared me in the face, suspended in mid-air, looking me straight in the eyes and saying, "What you throw you will keep!"

The Boomerang was taunting me guys.

REALLY?! I mean, *I* wrote the book! I should have been a better Boomerang Success Thinker.

You probably know what I mean. Staring face to face with a result that you hate, while also knowing that you yourself have created the result, is not fun! What happened? Well, as I've said before, the Boomerang Effect works. When you make a choice, you are choosing a Boomerang to throw and the Boomerang is going to fly back to you. In my case, I chose wrong.

My choice had to do with how I had been working on an ongoing assignment in school. The assignment was due and I took a good look at what my last few months of "work" had accomplished.

It wasn't a proud moment.

The Boomerang Effect is always at work though: *What you sow, you will reap. What you throw, you will keep.* It  always comes back! When I thought about my result and really analyzed it, I realized that I had chosen to throw the COMPROMISE-Boomerang instead of the EXCELLENCE-Boomerang. I took the easy way out and got the result that easy-way-out choices will get you.

I didn't like that result.

Team NEGATIVITY

→ **COMPROMISE**

BOOMERANG TO SUCCESS:

....

Stop blaming others for your results.

#TheBoomerangEffect

....

So what do you do when you know the COMPROMISE-Boomerang is staring you in the face with a Result that you hate? Own it. Stop blaming people for that result! Stop blaming the devil for that result! Stop blaming the weather, the government, the school or random situations. Stop blaming God for that result! Begin blaming *yourself*…but do it in a healthy way. Don't get all depressed and sad, own the result and move forward with a plan to not get the same bad result again.

Shatter Up!

Where you are today is a result of the Boomerangs you've thrown in the past. (Unless what you are in the middle of is something completely out of your control, like a health condition, a natural disaster, other family members' choices, etc.) I got behind in a subject because of the choices I made. I had to own that.

COMPROMISE IS LIKE A SNEAKY PREDATOR

The Boomerang I'd chosen to throw was called "Compromise" and it's like a sneaky predator. It hunts for a Weak Mindset. If you've thrown the COMPROMISE-Boomerang, it was a weakness in your mindset that talked you into choosing the wrong Boomerang. If you can begin to attack the weakness in your thinking that allowed the COMPROMISE-Boomerang to creep in and pounce, then you are making progress!

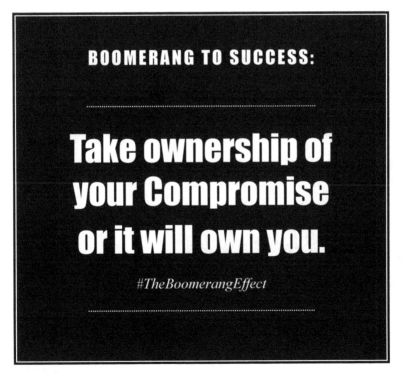

The Boomerang Effect, Malachi Walker | 129

The same Weak Mindset that helped you choose the COMPROMISE-Boomerang the first time will creep in again and pounce the next time you are choosing between Compromise and Excellence. Weak Mindset habits do not go away, they just get worse.

Unless you attack them!

SAVAGE-RESPONSE NOT AVERAGE-RESPONSE

Your response to Compromise must be strong. It must be swift. It must be focused and full of intention. It must be Savage. Strong like a lion. Swift like a cheetah. Focused like an eagle. Intentional like a wolf. Savage…like a Boomerang Mindset *Thinker.*

Boom!

When you understand that Compromise is hunting for a weak and average mindset to pounce on, then you will understand that you cannot be lazy in your response to fixing what caused your first Compromise. You must *not* give an Average-Response to the fail; you must give a SAVAGE-Response!

Team POSITIVITY

SAVAGE-RESPONSE ←

Figure out the weakness you have that helped you give in to the Compromise. Over the course of several months, I chose to throw the COMPROMISE-Boomerang as I worked towards a school project. When that came back and stared me in the face with the result, I knew I had to fix something. I hated the result. It set me back in several ways and required more time to fix than it would have taken to just do it right the first time.

A response is required. Whether you give a Savage-Response or an Average-Response, you will respond in some way. In my situation, an Average-Response would be to shrug my shoulders, feel bad about it, slowly work towards completing the assignment and not really look at *why* I chose Compromise instead of choosing Excellence.

NO! I don't want Average-Results so I cannot give Average-Responses! I refused to get the same result again, whether it would be in school, in the business I'm building, or in a relationship that's important to me. I needed a Savage-Response, which meant I needed to attack that Compromise mindset and fix it!

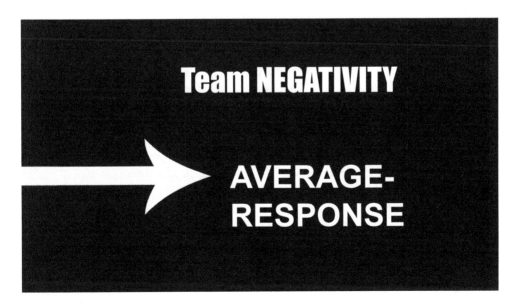

BOOMERANG TO SUCCESS:

....

If you don't want Average-Results, do not give Average-Responses!

#TheBoomerangEffect

....

When I attacked my Compromise, I figured out what started my Compromise. You see, that's what a Savage-Response will result in! You figure out "why" you gave in. You know, what starts Compromise is usually small and sneaky.

In my situation, I discovered that as I was focused on getting things ready for this book to launch, building a *YouTube* channel and planning out a business, I stopped making school a main goal. I thought, "It's OK. It'll get done. It's not my passion anyway and I don't want it to be my focus. It's just school—no big deal."

What kind of thinking is that?! It's thinking that encouraged Compromise not Excellence, that's what kind of thinking it was. That is not OK. I'm still in school and if I'm involved in something, I must choose to be excellent in it. I made a change. School must be a top priority, as well as my business! I cannot compromise that!

My Savage-Response to figuring out what was wrong about my thinking helped me make a positive change. I never would have made that discovery if I had taken an Average-Response to my Compromise. I'd be doing the same thing semester after semester and getting the same results. Even worse, the Compromise in one area of my goals would likely start to spill over into another area. Remember, Compromise is like a sneaky predator and it is never satisfied.

You must attack Compromise! Boomerang Mindset Thinkers cannot keep getting Average-Results. Be Savage about it! Go after the *reason* you chose wrong and get to work to fix it. How will you shatter a glass ceiling if you don't stare Compromise in the face and deal with it?!

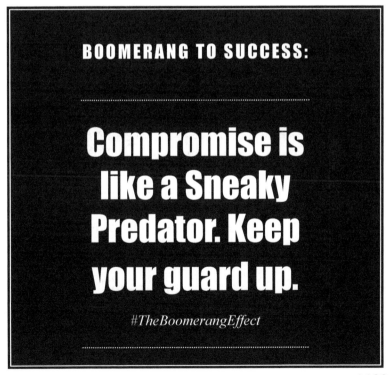

BOOMERANG TO SUCCESS:

Compromise is like a Sneaky Predator. Keep your guard up.

#TheBoomerangEffect

OWN IT AND MOVE ON

If you don't take a Savage-Response to dealing with the result of the COMPROMISE-Boomerang, you will fall into the trap of feeling sorry for yourself, sinking into a pit and moping around. Why? Because you are very aware that *you* are responsible for the bad result.

NO! You must not "throw" this Average-Response! It can slow you down for years, like a turtle. Some people never rebound. Say "sorry" if you need to, make things as right as you can, and then give a Savage-Response by training your Mindset. There *will* be a "next time." Compromise will creep in and want you to choose it, but "next time" you will be ready to choose the EXCELLENCE-Boomerang! Why?

Because you gave a Savage-Response to your Compromise and *that's* what *Boomerang Mindset Thinkers* do! Compromise must become *your* prey!!

THINK before you THROW. Excellence is always the better choice.

Some people are sidetracked for years from a negative result that was created when they threw the wrong Boomerang. This is because they chose the Average-Response towards their mistake. If you want an Average-Rebound from a mistake then yes, feel sorry for yourself, whine around and keep your weak mindset. You will be the prey of Compromise once again because your mindset towards Compromise hasn't changed any. But, if you want a Savage-Rebound from your mistake, you must give a Savage-Response and GET BACK UP, learn from your mistake, and move on.

Maybe you made an "honest mistake" when you threw the COMPROMISE-Boomerang. The Boomerang Effect is still at work though and a negative result will fly back. Sometimes you

Choose a Savage-Response to Compromise by fixing the weakness in your mind that helped you make the wrong choice.

#TheBoomerangEffect

really didn't mean to create a bad result, but it still slams into your stomach, and slams into your business, and slams into your future!

What have I done?!

The very next question should be, "What should I do now?!"

Pick up the SAVAGE-Boomerang and throw! Do not stay down! When a bad result hits you, don't focus on your mistake too much. Reflect on the reason you got the bad result, and move on to make up for what you've lost from that unexpected result. Have a Savage-Response and do a sit-up in your mind. Move forward!

If you accidentally throw a COMPROMISE-Boomerang, don't blame the negative result on someone else. That just makes it worse for you *and* them. Own it. Remind yourself that it was a Weak Mindset in that moment that helped you Compromise. Then choose to do differently next time.

STOP THROWING CARELESSLY!

Knowing how bad a negative result can feel, you should understand this point well: Do not choose a Boomerang carelessly and just hope for it to come back to you with a good result.

Careless choices often = Negative results.

Think about it. How many lives have texting and driving destroyed? How many families have drinking and driving torn apart? How many homes have burnt down because of an iron left on, a gas stove left burning or something simple like that? Careless choices hurt.

There's a good chance that careless choices will *not* come back to you with that great result you are expecting. Do not blame the Boomerang for a bad result! Blame yourself for choosing the Boomerang *carelessly.* But then be encouraged because your next step is: Get to work to change the mindset you had that helped you make a careless choice so you don't make it the next time.

The Average-Response to choosing a Boomerang is to choose it *carelessly.* Careless choices are thoughtless choices. You're not even thinking about your throw. What kind of coach wants an athlete on the field making careless plays? No coach wants that! Why would you want to be a careless decision maker? A careless Boomerang thrower? You are on Team Positivity!

Think before you throw. Be a Savage-Thrower, a Savage-Thinker!!

That's what my Boomerang Mindset Coach helps me to do! It's SAVAGE not AVERAGE. It's EXCELLENCE not COMPROMISE!

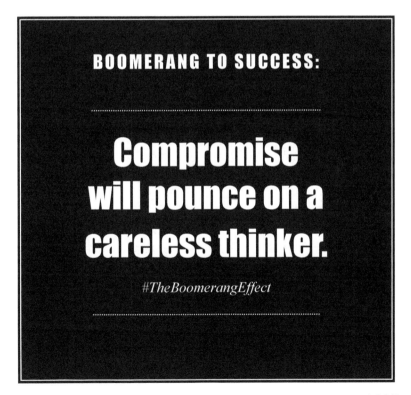

BOOMERANG TO SUCCESS:

Compromise will pounce on a careless thinker.

#TheBoomerangEffect

No more careless throws! Compromise will pounce on a careless thinker. Always throw the EXCELLENCE-Boomerang…it's the last thing Compromise thinks you will do. You are a *Boomerang Mindset Thinker* and YOU DON'T GIVE THE AVERAGE-RESPONSE! This team Stands Out, we Stand Up, and we are Different!

We think before we throw and we Shatter glass ceilings!

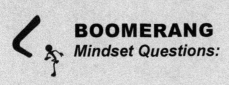

BOOMERANG
Mindset Questions:

1. Complete this phrase: "Compromise is like a
   _____   _____."
   Why is this true?

2. Describe a situation when you chose Compromise instead of Excellence.

3. What are some results of Compromise?

4. Look at the *Boomerang to Success* tips in this chapter. Choose one. How will you apply it?

#shatterup

THE CHEER-ON BOOMERANG

CHAPTER 9

Two questions:

1. Who are you a big fan of?
2. Who is *your* biggest fan?

Anyone can be a fan of anyone. That means you can have a fan! You don't have to be famous or wealthy to have a fan. So ask yourself, "Who should be my biggest fan?" There might be many people who would want to be your fan or there might not be, but there is one person who *needs* to be your biggest fan.

Your biggest fan should be YOU! Go ahead and go Wild, Yell, Jump, Clap and Cheer for YOURSELF!

Pick up the CHEER-ON Boomerang and yell something Positive at yourself! Let yourself hear *yourself* YELLING for yourself! Sounds crazy, but if you try it you will feel encouraged. Go crazy. Now.

"WOW!! Did you just see that? YES-I-DID! I ROCK!! YEAH! *BOOM!!"*

Go ahead. Try it!

....

You need to hear yourself cheering for yourself, because sometimes you won't hear anyone else cheering.

#TheBoomerangEffect

....

The CHEER-ON Boomerang means YOU open YOUR mouth and CHEER for your own accomplishment.

You might be wondering, "Why should I cheer myself on?"

Well, let's face the fact. It's very likely that there aren't many people cheering for you. Sometimes you will be the ONLY person who is cheering for you. That's why you have to cheer yourself on. This takes a Boomerang Success Mindset because you won't always *feel* like encouraging yourself, but that doesn't mean you do not *need* to be encouraged.

There will be times when you accomplish something great and there will be times when you fail at something greatly. If you don't have encouragement in *that* moment, you will get discouraged and maybe even depressed.

At that type of moment, you have two Boomerangs to pick from.

1. CHEER-ON Boomerang
2. TEAR-DOWN Boomerang

Why TEAR-DOWN? Because, at the moment you need to hear the CHEERS but you don't, you will feel disappointed and discouraged. The lack of Cheers for a job-well-done can actually

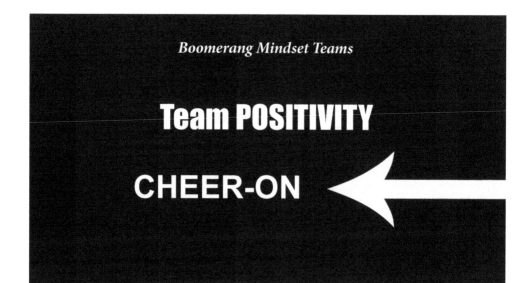

start to tear you down. Saying nothing can be good or bad. But saying nothing at the *wrong* time is bad and will tear down your Mindset.

Your mind must stay strong, so choose to throw the CHEER-ON Boomerang by opening your mouth and telling yourself what you know you need to hear. In those discouraging moments, it's so easy to start tearing yourself down with your own words. Stop that! Do not throw the TEAR-DOWN Boomerang. If you seem to have that bad habit when you're discouraged, recognize the pattern and *explode* it! *BOOM!* You can explode the pattern by picking up the CHEER-ON Boomerang, cheer for yourself and then keep on going forward!

If you want to be Successful, then you've chosen to be on Team POSITIVITY, but it doesn't mean you will always *want* to be positive. Be sure you are throwing for the right Team, especially if you feel discouraged. It can be hard, but remember that Mindset Conditioning is always worth it.

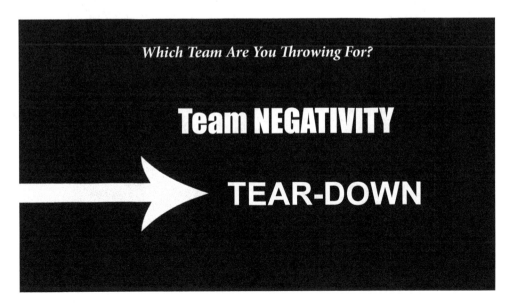

If you get discouraged and stay discouraged, you are trapping yourself under a glass ceiling. You will always Look-Up and wish on those stars, but you'll never Shatter-Up.

#TheBoomerangEffect

BOOMERANG MINDSET
SUCCESS STORY

One of my all-time favorite historical figures was a warrior and king named David. He was brave and fearless but there were still times when he had to choose the CHEER-ON Boomerang. (You can read this story in a book called the Bible in 1 Samuel 30.)

David and his men went out to fight a battle; they won it and took all the spoils! Then they returned to their camp to find the unimaginable. While they were away at battle, their camp had been raided, all their stuff had been stolen and their wives and families were gone! Talk about a bummer day.

People seem to always want to blame others for something bad, so the men blamed David. All of David's men wanted to kill him and I'm sure David didn't have anyone encouraging him at that moment...maybe encouraging him to jump off a cliff.

"David was greatly distressed because the men were talking of stoning him." (NIV 1 Sam. 30:6)." Things were not looking good. I mean, who wants to be stoned?! David could have sunk into a pit of despair. But what did he do? He threw a CHEER-ON Boomerang when NO ONE else was anywhere close to cheering him on.

It says that David got away by himself and "encouraged himself in the Lord," (verse six in the KJV). He had to pick up the CHEER-ON Boomerang. He had to get an answer about how to solve the problem and he had to be able to think straight so he could solve it. Throwing the TEAR-DOWN Boomerang would fly back to him and knock him out with discouragement. There was no time for that!

Once David cleared his mind enough to be able to think and pray to God, he asked if he should pursue the enemy. God told him "yes."

So David got his men together and they chased after the raiders. They caught up with them, beat them in battle and recaptured *everything!* BOOM!

All because of the Boomerang David chose to throw when he was discouraged!

But what if he had chosen to not pick up the CHEER-ON Boomerang and throw it? He would have stayed depressed and discouraged and probably would have gotten himself killed. David and his men would never have seen their wives or kids again. The stakes were high and the Boomerang choice was a *big* deal!

BOOMERANG TO SUCCESS:

You can't think straight when you are discouraged. Cheer yourself up first, then make the decision.

#TheBoomerangEffect

Negativity always wants to tear down the important things you have spent time building. So when you are in a Negative mindset, every choice is a TEAR-DOWN Boomerang. But David chose to throw for Team Positivity. David became his biggest fan…his only fan for that matter.

You know, even though that situation was as Negative as it could be, David chose NOT to throw with Team NEGATIVITY. But all of his men immediately switched right on over to Team NEGATIVITY and wanted to knock David out with all their NEGATIVE-Boomerangs. What kind of team was that?!

Don't be that kind of teammate. Please.

Those TEAR-DOWN Boomerangs were flying right back to them and they were about to commit murder, lose their children and wives forever, and all their belongings. Why? Because they were so overwhelmed with Negativity.

I'm sure glad they had a leader who was a Boomerang Mindset Thinker and who knew how to choose the right Boomerang even when it was really tough to choose it.

You cannot think straight when you're negative. It messes with your mind. David chose not to "catch" that Negative attitude and he stayed put on Team POSITIVITY.

No matter what you are dealing with, commit to Team POSITIVITY and it will work out. The Boomerang Effect is true: If you Sow POSITIVTY enough, you will REAP it and get back all your stuff! Just like David did.

SO ENCOURAGE YOURSELF

Sometimes in order to do your best, you will have to encourage YOURSELF.

You might be working out or trying to accomplish your goal and nobody's around to help you. You might be walking down the hallway, surrounded by a crowd, and have a huge challenge in front of you, but nobody is encouraging you. You might have finally accomplished a major step in your plan and no one seems to care or even understand what a big deal it is to you.

At those times, you're the *only* one who can cheer yourself on. And you need to, or you'll be throwing the TEAR-DOWN Boomerang. If you know you need to hear encouragement and nobody else is doing it, then YOU do it.

You do have a fan—it's YOU. Pick up the CHEER-ON Boomerang and throw it!

When nobody's around, if you don't cheer yourself on as you are working towards your goal, you will probably not do your very best…which means you won't *become* your best. Because the work you do when nobody is watching, is "the grind" that boosts you forward toward your goal. But if you don't do your best when nobody is watching, you will not be boosted forward.

So throw the CHEER-ON Boomerang! If you do not cheer yourself on, I don't believe you will accomplish smart, challenging or meaningful goals that bring out the best in you. Goals are hard; they take work and perseverance. It's too easy to give up. There will be moments when you don't have any encouragement and you have to reach inside yourself and find the encouragement. Be strong. Believe in yourself and cheer yourself on to the completion of your goal!

The next time you feel bad about something, cheer yourself up by finding something positive to focus on! It gets hard. You will want to quit. And you will feel like no one cares—sometimes they don't. But YOU care. You are your biggest FAN. Even if everyone around you starts throwing for the Wrong Mindset Team, cheer yourself on because *you* know which Team you are throwing for! Don't change

BOOMERANG TO SUCCESS:

The physical and mental work you do by yourself, when nobody else is watching, is work that boosts you forward towards your goal.

#TheBoomerangEffect

who you are just because it's hard—be like David and get back in the battle. You deserve to win!

THROW THE CHEER-ON BOOMERANG FOR OTHERS

Don't only cheer yourself on, cheer others on too! People like it when you cheer them on. When you are your biggest fan, you practice cheering all the time. That spills over like a full jug of water to other people and it begins to feel normal to cheer others on too!

They will want to listen to what you have to say. More people will want to connect with you, so that means you can impact more people! The more people who listen to you (as long as what you're saying has good value), the more people you influence in a good way. They will learn from you and start picking up POSITIVE-Boomerangs too. You will even get some new team members to switch over to Team POSITIVITY. Now you are changing the world!

If you have been throwing the CHEER-ON Boomerang when you needed your own encouragement, then you know how powerful it is. You can be that power for someone else! CHEER-ON others when you see a moment where they need it. And never throw the TEAR-DOWN Boomerang at others. *Why* do that? Try to always be Positive!

Cheer others on and *your* life will be impacted too. Cheer others on and they will cheer you on, and that will help you reach your goals! Sometimes you will want to quit, that is when your habit of cheering others on flies back to you, and they will cheer you on. Because when you plant seeds, they grow and come back to you—that is the Boomerang Effect! Their cheers might come at the exact moment you need to hear encouragement. That moment of encouragement could help you decide not to quit and it all started because you cheered someone else on.

When you cheer others on, you will feel better and they will too. An encourager attracts great moments! Try it and you will reach more of your goals, have more friends, get more business partners, have a better reputation, sell more of your product, have greater influence and be more successful. Plant positive seeds by throwing the CHEER-ON Boomerang!

CHEER-ON TRANSFORMERS

"More than meets the eye!" Do not only work towards transforming your life, also work on transforming others' lives. When you throw a CHEER-ON Boomerang for someone else, watch them change for the better—like a Transformer!

A lot of people think that being successful means having lots of money. That's a small part of what success is. But success is also having a lot of great advice, from your own experiences, that you can use to help others. If your advice helps take them to the next level, you have helped create success.

Your wisdom can transform how people think and how they work. So use the insights you have to help others accomplish their goals and not give up. When someone accomplishes a big goal and you have helped them, they shatter the glass and transform to the next level! You played a part because you chose to build and encourage by throwing the CHEER-ON Boomerang.

When I finish this book, I will transform to the next Level. I will still be Malachi Walker, but I will then be Malachi Walker, the Author. I will never *not* be an author for the rest of my life. My life will be transformed. And I couldn't have done it without my Boomerang Success Coaches tossing a lot of CHEER-ON Boomerangs my way! Their advice helped create my success and I Shattered-Up!

When you see someone who is about to quit, throw a CHEER-ON Boomerang by giving advice that you know will help them GET-UP. You might have already solved the type of problem they are trying to solve. Share your knowledge and throw a Cheer-On Boomerang their way!

It's simple, but it does more than you can imagine. Give cheers and encourage others! Who knows, you could save a person's life. What if *your* cheers help to stop someone from throwing the GIVE-UP Boomerang?! Now *that's* a big deal! Close the deal and help transform someone else's life by throwing the CHEER-ON Boomerang.

BOOMERANG TO SUCCESS:

It is better to give than to receive. Stop being stingy with your words of encouragement.

#TheBoomerangEffect

The more you transform others' lives, the more their success will help you transform yours. *What you sow, you will reap. What you throw, you will keep.* It may be hard at first to transform others' lives when you want to transform your own life so badly. But the Boomerang Success Mindset of cheering others on will return back to you and help you accomplish your goal!

As the World's #1 Wealth Coach, JT Foxx, says: "Powered by *your* success." Mr. JT always talks about the success of his clients and how the more successful they become, the more successful he becomes. That's the Boomerang Effect right there!

Throw the CHEER-ON Boomerang for others by giving them great advice. Give them what you have to give, because no one's goal is more important than another's. Help them reach their goal and they will help you reach your goal. You will help others be successful, which will give you power to become even more successful!

CHEER-ON Boomerangs transform things. David transformed complete defeat to complete victory because he chose the CHEER-ON Boomerang. Haven't you always wanted to be a Transformer?!

Pick up a Boomerang. It's time to Transform something and Shatter-Up!

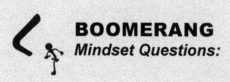

BOOMERANG
Mindset Questions:

1. Who is your favorite athlete or team? Why?

2. Who is *your* biggest fan? Who should it be?

3. Finish this *Boomerang to Success* Tip: "It's better to _____than to _____. Stop being _____with your words of _____."

4. How are CHEER-ON Boomerangs like Transformers?

#shatterup

Shatter Up!

YOUR FACE IS SPEAKING

CHAPTER 10

COMPLIMENTS ARE CHEER-ON BOOMERANGS

If you are throwing for Team POSITIVITY, then giving a Compliment needs to become a habit of yours. If a friend feels down in the dumps about something, cheer them up to the sky about something. Throw some Compliments their way with your words and with your facial expressions.

Your face is always speaking; it's always saying something.

Strengthen Team POSITIVITY by tossing out some COMPLIMENT-Boomerangs! And remember, the Boomerang Effect is at work, so those Compliments will come back to you with a positive result. *BOOM!*

But most people do the average thing. They *think* something Positive about someone else but they never say it or show it.

And, when they think something Negative about someone else, they *do* say it and they *do* show it. That's backwards, isn't it? It's an Average-Response to throw an Insult instead of a Compliment. People who do this are not Boomerang Success Thinkers…they need to condition.

Sometimes you will not *feel* like giving a Compliment. Remember, when you don't *feel* like throwing for Team POSITIVITY but you do it anyway, it's called Conditioning. Every time you do this, you are getting stronger and closer to Shattering some glass!

For example:

If you play baseball and your team loses (or your kid's team loses), find something positive that your team did and tell them. Do not throw a bunch of INSULT-Boomerangs because you are all mad about the loss. You are not considered to be a positive person if you have bad sportsmanship. Control your attitude! Good sportsmanship includes giving a Compliment. Tell the other team they did good. Throw the CHEER-ON Boomerang by giving a Compliment. Say it *and* show it. "Good game!"

Doing this does not mean that you are happy with the result of a loss. It just means you have enough self-control and maturity to see the big picture.

....

Pause and see the bigger picture. Then talk.

#TheBoomerangEffect

....

No, it's not easy! But when it's not easy, remember that you are CONDITIONING your mind. And you are not a whimp, so condition. Be thankful that you are playing a sport or (if you're an adult) that your child is playing a sport…or that they can play period. There are so many kids in hospitals looking out the window wishing they could do what you're doing.

Stop picking up a NEGATIVE-Boomerang so quickly! *Boomerang Success Thinkers* have this mindset: "What am I becoming because

SMILES are CHEER-ON Boomerangs:

SMILE ⟵

of this negative experience?" Start positive and stay positive. Giving Compliments will help you do this. Throw CHEER-ON Boomerangs. Do not change teams!

It's a choice. It's about what you are becoming—if you lost a game… or a deal, or a position, or your phone…what did you become because of the loss? Did you grow your skill of being able to think and speak positive even when you did not feel like it? Or did you start throwing Tear-Down Boomerangs with your words and attitude? See the obstacle as a way to condition your MINDSET.

"OK, yes this is a problem. No, I don't like it. But I'm going to become better because of this problem."

Always reach for a Team POSITIVITY-Boomerang: The CHEER-ON not the TEAR-DOWN, the GET-TO not the HAVE-TO, the BLESSED not the FRUSTRATED, and the SMILE not the FROWN. When you do this, you will Shatter your glass ceiling because you are using a strategy that works!

When people look at a person, usually the first thing they look at is their Face. Because most people look at your face before they look at anything else, you always need to have a good facial expression. First impressions make impressions. So your face is making an impression. (After they look at your face, they skip everything and look at your shoes. So make sure you've got some DOPE shoes on.)

You can automatically motivate and throw the CHEER-ON Boomerang by doing something as simple as smiling or even saying a little comment like, "Cool shoes."

But you know what? Most people are so stuck in their own heads that they reach for the FROWN-Boomerang and toss it. Ever wonder why there are so many people around you frowning? Because *you* did not throw a SMILE.

People usually respond to a FROWN with a FROWN. They see a sour face and it makes them feel sour. Choose to throw the SMILE-Boomerang. It will actually make you feel better too. And, more people will throw a SMILE back your way. *What you sow, you will reap. What you throw, you will keep.*

The SMILE-Boomerang comes back to you like one of those Hail Mary Catches made by a wide receiver. The FROWN-Boomerang flies back to you like a big smack down by the free safety. Do you want the touch down or the broken pass? SMILE. Nobody is too important that they cannot SMILE at others.

Turn that frown upside down.

If you always look positive, people will have an urge to be positive around you—remember the Boomerang Effect? People can tell what kind of person you are by just looking at your face. People will feel either Cheered-On or Torn-Down when they look at your Face.

So what's your face look like?

People who stay stuck at the same level wear lots of Frowns. If you are focusing on Shattering-Up, then there is an energy about you. You have a goal, a purpose and a Smile.

Think about it, emojis became popular because they said a lot without saying a word. What are you saying without saying a word? Throw the SMILE-Boomerang!

While you are at it, open your mouth and say something nice. The Compliment is another CHEER-ON Boomerang that many Average-Thinkers do not use. But you? You are a conditioned Boomerang Success Thinker! So you understand that Compliments

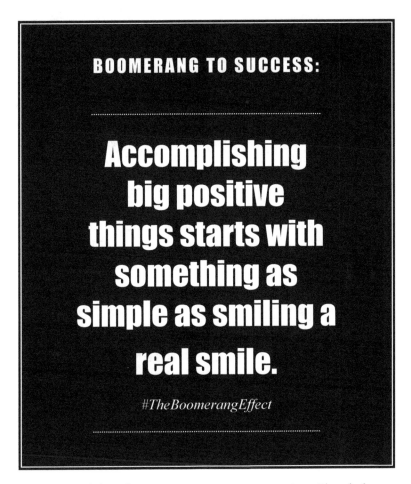

BOOMERANG TO SUCCESS:

Accomplishing big positive things starts with something as simple as smiling a real smile.

#TheBoomerangEffect

pave the road for what is to come in a conversation. They help you accomplish your goal and they help the listener receive the message you have for them.

Compliments also work great if you are asking your parents for a *Nintendo Switch* (just saying).

If having a positive facial expression and saying little comments to cheer others on can make such a huge difference, then why don't many people do it? Well, I'll tell you. Most people use one of two Excuses.

Excuse #1:

Smiling or Speaking a simple Compliment is "...too small to make a difference—it really doesn't matter." WRONG! Someone who says that is just lazy. If you are a Boomerang Success Thinker you are smart enough to know that if you can do something small and it make a BIG impact, *you* should do it! Just because you do not see value in doing something small, doesn't mean the small thing has no value. (Pause and think about that.)

Look at the small honeybee. Mess up the bee colony's pollination routine and you get a domino disaster for farmers and eventually the health of a nation. And, if a Smile or a simple Compliment is soooo small of a thing, then why don't you do it anyway?! What's the big deal? Put an X on that Excuse and do not use it. Turn it into an X-Use!

BOOMERANG TO SUCCESS:

....

Your face is constantly speaking.

#TheBoomerangEffect

....

Excuse #2:

"I don't *feel* like it." Guess what? Your feelings are wrong. Push through. *You* are on Team POSITIVITY, not Team WHINING. You will like the results! I don't *feel* like being nice to people all the time. And sometimes I'm not—I'm working on that. But I cannot excuse my attitude with, "Well, I didn't *feel* like it." That's a wimpy excuse. Put an X on it! I will stop using it and you stop too. It will take some Mindset Conditioning, but I know we can do it!

Throw CHEER-ON Boomerangs constantly by always having a good facial expression. When people look at your face, they should know you are a Positive person! They should feel Positivity and they should feel Cheered-On! Giving others Compliments instead of Insults will come back to you as success. The little things can make a **BIG** difference.

Do the little things. Enough little things can shatter the glass that is containing you and move you to the next level!

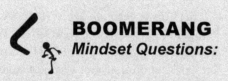

BOOMERANG
Mindset Questions:

1. Name two people who have cheered you on during a tough time.

2. When was the last time you were pumped about something you accomplished?

3. Name two ways that you can encourage others.

4. Look at the person next to you and SMILE. Now, SCOWL. (If you are not in a group setting, do this by yourself. Look in the mirror or just do it.) Which expression makes you feel better?

#shatterup

TAKE
THE SHOT

CHAPTER 11

Have you ever really wanted to try something but you chose not to? I think everybody has experienced that sinking feeling before. It's the feeling you get when you would love to give something a shot, but right away, you talk yourself out of it. Why do people talk themselves out of something that they know in their hearts they want to do?

People are too concerned about what others think, they are too concerned about failing, or they are too concerned about commitment so they just don't try. Excuses! Wouldn't it be better to actually try and fail than to always wish you *would* have tried? If you do not try, all chances are gone! You will forever be hitting your head on the glass ceiling that is keeping you at your current level—that's just not smart.

MAJOR POTENTIAL = MAJOR NOTHING

Let's say Lionel Messi and I, Malachi Walker, are both standing on the soccer field at mid-field. We both get one chance to shoot the ball from the exact same place using the exact same ball...I'm sure you've already decided who is going to win this.

Messi is one of the best soccer players on earth…possibly the best soccer player of all time. He has major *potential* to make it perfectly in the corner of the net from mid-field. At the current moment I have, let's say, minor potential. But Messi makes a decision that removes all of his potential from the equation. When it's his turn to take the shot, he just walks off the field.

BOOMERANG TO SUCCESS:

The goal is there, but if you never take the shot, the goal will never be scored.

#TheBoomerangEffect

What?! Why would he do that?

I take my shot but Messi does not take his shot. Who has a better chance of making the goal? Messi, with his major potential, or me with my current minor potential?

Well, I do! Why? Because I actually stay on the field and use my potential. Simply trying gives me an advantage over one of the top soccer players on Earth. I tried and won because I had no competition. Messi lost, he didn't even touch the ball. He was DQ'd.

Major Potential = Major Nothing if you do not try.

Major Nothing is the normal result for most people. Are you one of them? Are you standing at "mid-field" with major potential but you've just made the choice to turn around and walk off the field? If you do that, you are reaching down and picking up the IMPOSSIBLE-Boomerang. You kill all your chances when you pick up this Boomerang because *all* potential is lost.

Do something different if you want a different result! Instead, reach for the POTENTIAL-Boomerang. Throwing the POTENTIAL-

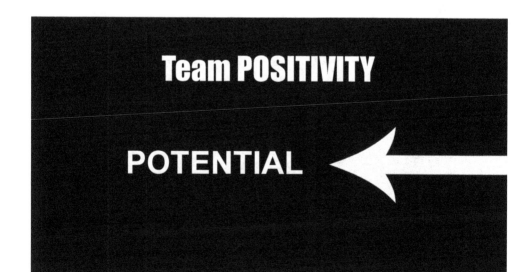

Boomerang doesn't mean it's automatic success, but it means that you are at least giving yourself a *chance* at success.

Be done with the "What if…" statement and get an answer. If you try and it does not work out, well at least you know. Give your idea life. Let it live, see what happens!!

To score a soccer goal you must put the ball in the goal, it's that simple. A soccer ball cannot move by itself. If you do not move it, you cannot score.

You may even have more potential to succeed then the pros had when they decided to go after their goal, but if you never take a risk and try then you're going to get the average result…which is Major *Nothing.* Though you could be the best, you never will be. Though you could have a business, you never will. Though you could get involved in a cause, you will not because you won't take the shot. You must *move* the ball. You have to throw the POTENTIAL-Boomerang!

Major Potential means nothing if you do nothing with it! Go ahead and pick up the IMPOSSIBLE-Boomerang because that is all you're going to get if you walk off the field and don't "take the shot."

Stop losing by choice.

BOOMERANG TO SUCCESS:

....

Every shot that is not taken is missed.

#TheBoomerangEffect

....

Most kids believe they are going to do or be something amazing… and they should! But most kids never do those big things or become those big ideas. Why? They never really try. A dream stays a dream until someone says, "I'm going to take the shot." I could have dreamed and dreamed about being an author but I would have accomplished a Major Nothing.

Lots of steps must be taken to "score a goal." I think most adults stop when they have taken one or two steps and then realize the goal requires so much more. Most kids stop because they take one or two steps and then do not know what to do because they don't have some sort of coach to help them. Both adults and kids throw the POTENTIAL-Boomerang a few times…but soon they pick up the IMPOSSIBLE-Boomerang and throw it. Then, all the potential is lost, because they walk off the field.

DO NOT WALK OFF THE FIELD.

Fear causes you to walk off the field. Don't be afraid of failing. Take the shot and have faith that you will make it! If you fail, it will actually make you braver, because at least you knocked out fear and took the shot. So either way, it comes back to you as success because you get better!

If you try and fail, you still threw the POTENTIAL-Boomerang so POTENTIAL flies back to you. Great things can come from a failed goal. This is a Mindset Conditioning opportunity! You get stronger, you learn what works and what does not. Now you have more knowledge for your next shot.

The big problem happens when you choose to not even try. Why is it a big problem? Because when you do not try, you choose to throw the IMPOSSIBLE-Boomerang and your only result will be *nothing.* The IMPOSSIBLE-Boomerang does not have potential. You throw IMPOSSBILE and you reap something called: NOTHING. You gain nothing and you learn nothing, except how to *not* believe in yourself and how to *not* take chances at success.

Why do so many people choose to throw the IMPOSSIBLE-Boomerang?

I think they have a fear of failure, but they will not call it a fear. Most people who have failed will often *not* try new things because they are afraid to fail again. But that's the wrong way to look at something. If you try and fail, you must remind yourself of this: "When I tried, I picked up the POTENTIAL-Boomerang!" What does that mean? It means that even if you failed at your goal, POTENTIAL is flying back to you. CATCH IT! Then use it to give yourself a better chance at your goal the next time around. Failure can boomerang back to you as success!

BOOMERANG TO SUCCESS:

Choose to have faith that a positive result will happen next time, instead of having fear that a negative result will happen.

#TheBoomerangEffect

BOOMERANG MINDSET
SUCCESS STORY

My mom is a vocal performance coach. One of her students, Amyah Velazquez, tried out for *The Voice*. She didn't make it all the way through but she is an *amazing* singer! She's only thirteen. You know, Amyah could have sat at home while the other thousands of people went to give it a try. She could have talked herself out of it and focused on the fact that the chances of making it are miniature. So why even try?

But Amyah chose to throw the POTENTIAL-Boomerang. Though she didn't make it through on her first shot, POTENTIAL flew back to her! The experience she gained just by taking the shot is going to boost her forward faster than others who didn't try.

"Amyah Velazquez." You should follow her career. She won't give up. Amyah is another youth trying to shatter her glass ceiling and go to the next level. So I say, "Do it! Go Shatter-Up!"

WHY WON'T YOU TAKE THE SHOT?

Whatever "take the shot" means for you, take it! It could be sports, acting, singing, game designing, cooking, building, speaking, teaching, YouTubing, training, investing, selling…whatever your thing is…TAKE THE SHOT!

A lot of people think, "If I don't try, I won't fail. And I do not want to fail, so I'm just not going to try. Problem solved!"

WHAT?!

Every time you will not try something that could help you reach your goal, you are failing anyway! So get over it and at least give the ball a *chance* to roll into the goal.

I'm not just talking about soccer here; I'm talking about your life goals! A goal cannot be reached by itself. It needs you to race towards it. To kick it. To push for it. To try!

BOOMERANG TO SUCCESS:

....

No goal can be reached if no one will reach for it.

#TheBoomerangEffect

....

Don't *not* try!! If the reason you will not try is because you are afraid of failing, then you've made your fear come true. You will auto-fail because you will not try. Remember, the ball cannot move by itself—it needs YOU. Don't be afraid to take a shot at the goal that is in your mind!! The ball is sitting there on the field. You auto-fail if you do not kick it. You miss every shot you never take. At least give yourself a chance.

Stop feeding the IMPOSSIBLE monster.

If you are a Boomerang Success Thinker, then you are on Team Positivity! When you have an opportunity to try something, you are either going to pick up the POTENTIAL-Boomerang or the

IMPOSSIBLE-Boomerang. How do you know which one you are going to choose? I think it has a lot to do with how you see failure.

FAILURE IS LOADED WITH POTENTIAL

So now is a good time to stop and ask yourself what you think about failure: What is failure? Does failure help you or hurt you? I think it does both. Failure helps you because it will put you through Mindset Conditioning and you can learn a lot from it; it hurts because no one likes when his or her idea, goal, dream or work does not equal success. People who get average results likely only see failure as something bad. But if you are someone who is trying to become successful, you know that failure can actually help you… it has POTENTIAL!

Failure may be a setback at first—like a knockdown. But if you use failure to help yourself grow, you can sit up from that knockdown. When you sit up from a knockdown, you sit up with more fire than you had *before* you were knocked down. *BOOM!*

Learn from failure! Failure is an obstacle, but if you grow from your failures, those failures will be opportunities that lead you to success. Failure is FULL of Potential! Like a water-balloon that is so full it's ready to burst at any second. Remember, you must throw the POTENTIAL-Boomerang in order to get any type of good result. If your result is a Fail, do the Mindset Conditioning and choose to remind yourself that your Fail is stuffed with POTENTIAL! Like these famous examples:

Walt Disney, founder of the Walt Disney Company, was fired by the Kansas City Star paper and his first animation business ended in bankruptcy = FAIL.

Oprah Winfrey, the TV icon, was told she was unfit for television = FAIL.

Michael Jordan, perhaps the greatest basketball player ever, was cut from his high school basketball team = FAIL.

Jack Ma, founder of Alibaba (The Amazon of China), failed middle school, was the sole reject among 24 applicants at KFC, and was rejected by Harvard 10 times = FAIL

What do these four very successful people have in common? They all realized that their Failures were full of Potential, so they picked up the POTENTIAL-Boomerang, threw again and eventually SHATTERED their glass ceilings! *BOOM!*

And on to the next level they went.

Who is your favorite successful person on the planet? What was one of their failures? Just google it, I'm sure you will land on something they failed at. I promise you that everyone who has become successful has had failure, but they were still able to become successful. Why? Because they treated their obstacles like opportunities and chose to believe that their fail was full of Potential. If you treat obstacles like opportunities, you can turn the bad around to be good, just like every successful person in the world has done.

Do not reach for the IMPOSSIBLE-Boomerang and just give up. What if Disney, Oprah, Jordan or Jack Ma chose to throw the IMPOSSIBLE-Boomerang after they tried and failed? You wouldn't know their names and they would never have reached their full potential. But they didn't reach for the IMPOSSIBLE-Boomerang after they failed. Instead, they reached again for the POTENTIAL-Boomerang and let it fly!

Now, that choice right there is a result of Mental Conditioning. Remember, hard mindset choices are not easy—do not expect them to be.

BOOMERANG TO SUCCESS:

If you Shatter-Up enough times, you will be at the top.

#TheBoomerangEffect

BOOMERANG TO SUCCESS:

Stop wanting it to be so easy.

#TheBoomerangEffect

What failure do you need to treat like an opportunity that is full of Potential? What shot have you not taken that has been missed, just because you didn't take it?

Why? Because it is IMPOSSIBLE.

Always remember this Boomerang to Success Tip:

THE GOAL IS THERE, BUT IF YOU NEVER TAKE THE SHOT, THE GOAL WILL NEVER BE SCORED.

A ball will not roll by itself. Put on your cleats and take the shot! What if the next "shot" you take is the one that shatters the glass ceiling that has been keeping you at the same level for so long? What if your shattered ceiling is connected to you walking back on the field, one more time, and choosing to try again?

Go ahead—put your cleats on and get back out there!

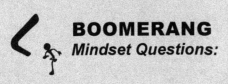

BOOMERANG
Mindset Questions:

1. Who is your favorite successful person? Why?

2. Name one thing that you are avoiding trying again. Why are you avoiding it?

3. Describe an opportunity you missed because you did not "Take The Shot."

4. What are three key lessons you can learn from a failure?

#shatterup

SHATTER UP

CHAPTER 12

Simon Chose the POTENTIAL-Boomerang

There is a story about some fishermen who went out to fish one night (NIV Luke 5:1-11). They fished the entire night and caught nothing. Nothing! Two boats were working together—it was their job, their business. The entire night they were throwing their nets overboard, hauling the nets back into the boat and hoping for fish but…nothing. No profit. Only work, sweat, stink and cost. Over and over again, they tossed those nets and…nothing.

They kept taking the shot, but never scoring a goal. Morning came and they were tired of hitting their heads on the glass ceiling. Game over. Let's go home. Throw the IMPOSSIBLE-Boomerang and get it over with. They pulled their boats up to shore, got out of the boat and went to clean their nets so they could go home and take a shower.

Right when they were throwing the IMPOSSIBLE-Boomerang, this man named Jesus showed up. He was walking on shore and there were a ton of people following Him to listen to Him talk. If they had cell phones back in those days, everyone would have been filming—this man was famous. They were in his face, so close they could take a selfie, and He needed space. Jesus saw Simon's boat, one of those fishermen who had fished all night, and climbed in. Then He asked Simon to push back a little from the shore so he could sit down and keep on speaking to the crowd...without feeling crowded.

Simon didn't know who this man was, but there was a crowd who wanted the man's attention and the man was talking to him. So Simon, who was tired and ready to go home, called to some of his business partners to help him and they pushed away from shore. Soon Jesus looked at Simon and said, "Put out into the deep water, and lower your nets for a haul."

I am sure Simon was thinking, "A haul? Are you kidding me?!" Simon was tired, worn out, done. He told Jesus, "...we toiled all night, exhaustingly, and caught nothing in our nets." He did not want to go through the process of lowering his net again! Neither did the other guys on the boat. WHY? They had already tried, tried hard. There was no Leveling Up that happened last night and no shattered ceiling for their business. They had already accepted the defeat, washed their nets and were ready to go home.

But then, Simon reaches for the *right* boomerang and it makes all the difference. He says this, "...we caught nothing in our nets, but on the ground of Your word, I will lower the nets again."

Why in the world would he do that?! I mean, would you do that? What made it worth it? It's not like putting keys into a car, turning it on and zooming 3 minutes up the road to the store. Simon had to raise the sails (that he had just lowered), get the nets back out (that he had just cleaned), spend time sailing out to the deep (where he had just spent the entire night), lower the nets again (which meant he would have to clean them out again), and...you get the picture. I'm sure the Excuses were stacking up fast in Simon's mind.

But Boomerang Mindset Thinkers put an X on Excuses and turn them into X-Uses!

And that's what Simon did. I think he decided to take one more

BOOMERANG TO SUCCESS:

Do not miss your next big moment because you are hung up on the disappointment of your last try.

#TheBoomerangEffect

shot because he was a Boomerang Mindset Thinker. He knew the power of the POTENTIAL-Boomerang. He decided to look at this last net-tossing like someone who was on Team Positivity.

Throwing the net one more time would at least give him one last chance at making something out of a zero-profit day of business. He had a hunger to Shatter his business ceiling and Level Up. The water was the same, the boat, nets and sails were the same, but someone different was on his boat. What if something about this man named Jesus was the factor he needed for catching fish that day?

Like an X-factor.

But it does not matter if you have the X-factor on your boat if you will not take the shot! The X-factor has to have something to work with. And Simon decided to give it something to work with—he gave it another shot! This proves he was on Team Positivity. He was not ready to give up. He wanted the result. He wanted the success! So he picked up the POTENTIAL-Boomerang again and tossed his net.

You know, it was just one more try. Just one more shot. But with that last shot, the Boomerang came back as Success! It's the Boomerang Effect: *What you sow, you will reap. What you throw, you will keep.*

Simon and the others lowered the net again using the same motions, same net and same boat they had used all night. But the result was not the same. Simon began to feel the net tug and soon, the net was so full of fish that the net began to break. They started signaling to their biz partners in the other boat to come help them! The other boat came to help and they "...filled both boats so full that they began to sink."

I can hear the glass ceiling Shattering now. *BOOM!* The boats were so full of fish, so full of profit that the boats began to sink. I am thinking that Simon and his business partners were rather glad he chose to throw the POTENTIAL-Boomerang just one more time.

Simon could have said, "NO! I'm not lowering that net again!" But he was a Boomerang Mindset Thinker like you and I are! We do not throw IMPOSSIBLE—we throw POTENTIAL! *What you sow, you will reap. What you throw, you will keep.* And on that day, with that last throw, he was finally successful!

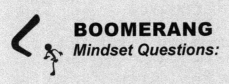

BOOMERANG
Mindset Questions:

1. What is the definition of "potential?"

2. What are two reasons that people limit their potential?

3. What did you take away from the story about Simon?

4. As a Boomerang Mindset Thinker, what will you do now to activate your Potential?

#shatterup

TO GO TO A NEW LEVEL YOU
MUST SHATTER YOUR CEILING

In the story of Simon and the big catch, someone saw the result that Simon could not see. Jesus saw the glass ceiling that was so close to shattering. He saw what was on the return of the next throw—if only Simon would pick up the FAITH-Boomerang and throw for Team Positivity *one* more time. Maybe Jesus knew the water current had shifted, maybe he had some insight the fishermen did not have...who knows? Whatever the reason for the big catch, it took something different to get a different result. And, it took one more throw of the POTENTIAL-Boomerang.

Maybe *The Boomerang Effect* has landed in your hands at this time in your life because some of the next "throws" in your life are more important than you even know. I know I'm only thirteen and I'm telling you how to think, but who cares?! What if this book changes your life? Your life, your family and your business can go to the next level by using *The Boomerang Effect* as your new standard for making choices. Let this book jump into your boat!

It is time to shatter the glass ceiling that you keep hitting your head on. Throw for Team Positivity and let *The Boomerang Effect* principle cause success to fly back to you! It works—it's time for you to work it and Level Up!

Can you feel it? Can you feel your heart beating faster and your mind racing? This is for you! The time is NOW. Leveling up is something that sounds great but it cannot just be an expression. This book is telling you *how* to level up. Boomerang Mindset Thinkers know that you cannot just *want* to level up, you must know *how* to and then you must take action and do it.

Here is how—short, sweet and simple. To level up, you must Shatter the ceiling that is holding you at your current level. You have to *SHATTER UP!* To Shatter Up you must use *The Boomerang Effect.*

To level up, you must Shatter the ceiling that is holding you at your current level. You have to SHATTER UP!

#TheBoomerangEffect

You have read the book—now do something! Now is the time to become a *Boomerang Mindset Thinker!* Now is the time to throw for Team Positivity! Now is the time to choose GET-UP instead of GIVE-UP! To choose X-USES instead of EXCUSES. To choose BLESSED instead of FRUSTRATED. To choose POTENTIAL instead of IMPOSSIBLE, to choose POSITIVITY instead of NEGATIVITY! To choose SAVAGE not AVERAGE! Now is the time to choose *THE BOOMERANG EFFECT.*

Pick up your Boomerang, it's time to throw!

BOOMERANG TO SUCCESS:

You never know which throw will Shatter your glass ceiling.

#TheBoomerangEffect

The Boomerang Effect:
What you sow, you will reap.
What you throw, you will keep.

BOOMERANG TO SUCCESS TIPS

BOOMERANG TO SUCCESS #1
Setbacks in life can be like sit-ups for the mind, so it's not really a setback. (p. 19)

BOOMERANG TO SUCCESS #2
When a Setback happens, do a Sit-up in your mind. Choose the GET-UP Boomerang and not the GIVE-UP Boomerang. The new mindset will boost you forward farther than you fell back. (p. 21)

BOOMERANG TO SUCCESS #3
Get Back Up and throw the Boomerang with passion again, no matter what is standing in your way. (p. 29)

BOOMERANG TO SUCCESS #4
No one can make you get back up. YOU must CHOOSE to. (p. 31)

BOOMERANG TO SUCCESS #5
Combine the good things from Adult-Thinking, Kid-Thinking, and Baby-Thinking to create Boomerang Success Thinking! (p. 42)

BOOMERANG TO SUCCESS #6
*Make up your mind that being Positive
will always give you the best result. (p. 50)*

BOOMERANG TO SUCCESS #7
*Set your mind on the right thought-track,
this way your thoughts will go in the right
direction. (p. 52)*

BOOMERANG TO SUCCESS #8
*Decide to be a POSITIVE PERSON and it will
help you see the big picture. Your life will change
for the better. (p. 55)*

BOOMERANG TO SUCCESS #9
Change the words "HAVE TO" into "GET TO."
× HAVE-TO ✓ GET-TO (p. 60)

BOOMERANG TO SUCCESS #10
*The Boomerang will fly back to you with the
same attitude you threw it with. (p. 63)*

BOOMERANG TO SUCCESS #11
*Complaining should never be
an option in your mind. (p. 67)*

BOOMERANG TO SUCCESS #12
*Every time you use an Excuse, you weaken your
own mind. Put an X on the Excuse and get
your strong mind back! (p. 79)*

BOOERANG TO SUCCESS #13
Most Excuses sound LOGICAL. (p. 83)

BOOMERANG TO SUCCESS #14
Excuses help you lie to yourself.
Then you are living a lie and
you think it is true. (p. 86)

BOOMERANG TO SUCCESS #15
Mindset Conditioning will make your physical
work easier and more productive. (p. 93)

BOOMERANG TO SUCCESS #16
Some of the hardest work you will ever do
is in your mind. (p. 96)

BOOMERANG TO SUCCESS #17
Ideas are easy, but goals are not.
Goals demand Commitment. (p. 98)

BOOMERANG TO SUCCESS #18
Stop treating hurdles like obstacles a
nd start treating them like opportunities. (p. 101)

BOOMERANG TO SUCCESS #19
That one chunk of work that some people
do once a week needs to be done every day.
Be consistent! (p. 103)

BOOMERANG TO SUCCESS #20
Your goal is right in front of you. But when you
spin in a circle, 99% of what you see is not your
goal; only 1% of what you see is your goal. Focus
on your GOAL! (p. 106)

BOOMERANG TO SUCCESS #21
There are many steps to get to the prize
that is way up there. Stay focused. (p. 107)

BOOMERANG TO SUCCESS #22
Mindset Conditioning is not easy.
But easy things do not shatter glass. (p. 123)

BOOMERANG TO SUCCESS #23
Stop blaming others for your results. (p. 128)

BOOMERANG TO SUCCESS #24
Take ownership of your Compromise
or it will own you. (p.129)

BOOMERANG TO SUCCESS #25
If you don't want Average-Results,
don't give Average-Responses! (p. 132)

BOOMERANG TO SUCCESS #26
Compromise is like a Sneaky Predator.
Keep your guard up. (p. 133)

BOOMERANG TO SUCCESS #27
Choose a Savage-Response to Compromise
by Fixing the weakness in your mind
that helped you make the wrong choice. (p. 135)

BOOMERANG TO SUCCESS #28
Compromise will pounce
on a careless thinker. (p. 137)

BOOMERANG TO SUCCESS #29
You need to hear yourself cheering for yourself,
because sometimes you won't hear anyone else
cheering. (p. 143)

BOOMERANG TO SUCCESS #30
If you get discouraged and stay discouraged,
you are trapping yourself under a glass ceiling.
You'll always Look-Up and wish on those stars,
but you'll never Shatter-Up. (p. 146)

BOOMERANG TO SUCCESS #31
You can't think straight when you are
discouraged. Cheer yourself up first,
then make the decision. (p. 148)

BOOMERANG TO SUCCESS #32
The physical and mental work you do by yourself,
when nobody else is watching, is work that boosts
you forward towards your goal. (p. 151)

BOOMERANG TO SUCCESS #33
It is better to give than to receive.
Stop being stingy with your words
of encouragement. (p. 154)

BOOMERANG TO SUCCESS #34
Pause and see the bigger picture. Then talk.
(p. 160)

BOOMERANG TO SUCCESS #35
Accomplishing big positive things starts with
something as simple as smiling a real smile.
(p. 163)

BOOMERANG TO SUCCESS #36
Your face is constantly speaking. (p. 164)

BOOMERANG TO SUCCESS #37
The goal is there, but if you never take
the shot, the goal will never be scored. (p. 169)

BOOMERANG TO SUCCESS #38
Every shot that is not taken is missed. (p. 172)

BOOMERANG TO SUCCESS #39
Choose to have faith that a positive result will happen next time, instead of having fear that a negative result will happen. (p. 174)

BOOMERANG TO SUCCESS #40
*No goal can be reached
if no one will reach for it. (p. 176)*

BOOMERANG TO SUCCESS #41
*If you Shatter-Up enough times,
you will be at the top. (p. 179)*

BOOMERANG TO SUCCESS #42
Stop wanting it to be so easy. (p. 180)

BOOMERANG TO SUCCESS #43
*Do not miss your next big moment
because you are hung up on the
disappointment of your last try. (p. 186)*

BOOMERANG TO SUCCESS#44
*To level up, you must Shatter the ceiling
that is holding you at your current level.
You have to SHATTER UP! (p. 191)*

BOOMERANG TO SUCCESS #45
*You never know which throw
will Shatter your glass ceiling. (p. 192)*

WORKS CITED

Introduction
"principle." en.oxforddictionaries.com. Oxford University Press, 2018. Web. 1 Aug 2016.

Chapter 3: BOOMERANG MINDSET TEAMS
Gordon, Jeff. The Positive Dog. Hoboken, NJ: John Wiley & Sons, Inc., 2012.

Chapter 6: MINDSET CONDITIONING: STEPS-TO-SUCCESS
"perseverance." en.oxforddictionaries.com. Oxford University Press, 2018. Web. 12 Oct 2016.

Chapter 9: The CHEER-ON BOOMERANG
NIV 1 Samuel 30:6. The Bible App. Version 8.3.4. App, New International Version.

Chapter 12: SHATTER UP
NIV Luke 5:1-11. The Bible App. Version 8.3.4. App, New International Version.

ABOUT THE AUTHOR

Malachi Walker lives in Dallas, TX. He is a 13-year old author, speaker, and entrepreneur who is passionate about personal growth, helping others achieve their goals, and serving God with his gifts and talents. He brings an electric atmosphere to his stages and has a unique ability to connect with his audience, both young and old.

After being sidelined with a potentially career-ending condition, Malachi made a choice that changed his life forever. From that choice, THE BOOMERANG EFFECT was born. This teen lives life with a purpose-driven enthusiasm like none other. As an eighth grade homeschooler, Malachi is a dedicated and disciplined student who enjoys football and loves playing for his Select soccer team. He also enjoys spending time with his family, leading at his church, and creating motivational content for his fans, "The MalaCrew". He'd love for you to connect with him on Facebook, YouTube, Twitter and Instagram.

Follow Malachi Walker:

BeyondPublishing.net/AuthorMalachiWalker
Facebook.com/MalachiWalker
Instagram.com/TheMalachiWalker
Twitter.com/theMalachiW

NOTES

#shatterup

NOTES

#theboomerangeffect

 **NOTES**

#shatterup

NOTES

#*theboomerangeffect*

Follow Malachi Walker:

BeyondPublishing.net/AuthorMalachiWalker
Facebook.com/MalachiWalker
Instagram.com/TheMalachiWalker
Twitter.com/theMalachiW

CPSIA information can be obtained
at www.ICGtesting.com
Printed in the USA
LVHW02s0222210818
587605LV00017B/336/P